And You Thought You Knew Classic Movies!

And You Thought You Knew Classic Movies!

A QUIZ BOOK

by John DiLeo

St. Martin's Griffin   New York

All photos courtesy of Photofest.

Library of Congress Cataloging-in-Publication Data

DiLeo, John, 1961–
    And you thought you knew classic movies! : a quiz book /
by John DiLeo.
        p.   cm.
    ISBN 0-312-19966-X
        1. Motion pictures—United States—Miscellanea. I. Title.
    PN1993.85.D56   1999   98-41595
    791.43'0973—dc21   CIP

First St. Martin's Griffin Edition: March 1999

10 9 8 7 6 5 4 3 2 1

TABLE OF CONTENTS

ACKNOWLEDGMENTS

Sincerest thanks to Naomi Wittes Reichstein, Cal Morgan, Anne Savarese, Richard Parks, Jerry Vermilye, Shira Levin, Randy Buck, Marty Jones, Clay Guthrie, Helen Silano, Julissa Santos, Alex Caliendo, Cynthia Sealy, Pauline Kael, my brother Michael, and my ever-patient partner, Earl McCarroll.

Colossal thanks to Tony Razzano and Maureen Caliendo.

AUTHOR'S NOTE

I was born in 1961 and immediately went to the movies. I was raised on the musical blockbusters of the sixties (a mixed blessing) and thought that Julie Andrews was in *all* movies (which was fine with me). And yet, it was the old movies on television that truly entranced me. In the pre-VCR mid-seventies, I was the kid who set his alarm clock for 2 A.M. on school nights so I could get up and watch *To Each His Own* or *Words and Music*. The ushers got to know me by name when I saw *That's Entertainment!* thirteen times in the summer of 1974.

My grandmother once described the movies of her youth by saying "they took you to another world." While today's movies are still capable of transporting us, the films of the Golden Age were generally at a farther remove from life as we know it. Someone can watch *All About Eve* or *The Philadelphia Story* and say that people don't really talk like that, but wouldn't it be a more scintillating world if they did? I guess that sense of a heightened reality is what makes the period so hypnotic. Does color exist in nature the way it does in *Cover Girl*? Did you ever meet anyone like Garbo?

It was my parents and grandparents who first exposed me to everything from the toughest John Garfield picture to the frothiest Esther Williams extravaganza. Born on an Oscar night, my mother, Vera, would dress up to watch the Oscar telecasts when she was a teenager. I'd like to thank her and my father, John, for opening up this joyful and enriching world to a boy who continues to treasure it.

John DiLeo

"RULES OF THE GAME"

This book covers movies up until the time I can remember going to them myself (mid to late sixties). I occasionally use more recent films, but only when there is a direct link to an older film or a studio-system star.

The quizzes are organized by category rather than difficulty, so don't be discouraged if you find some of the early ones hard to finish (you may sail through later chapters).

There is no disrespect intended toward any favorites of yours that I may have neglected (*Casablanca* gets only two mentions). Certain films simply fit better into the quiz topics than others (you may end up thinking *Spellbound* is one of my favorites, but it isn't).

Each correct answer is worth one point. There are ten points to be had in each of the 200 quizzes. However, sprinkled throughout are 166 extra-credit questions where I ask for additional information, such as "Then name the film." So, a perfect score is actually 2166. Don't forget these extra points when you add up your total. You'll find the scoring key after the answers section.

J.D.

Joseph Cotten and Teresa Wright in *Shadow of a Doubt*

ONE

"Imitation of Life"

1. Match the surprising first name (or nickname) of a screen character to the actress who played her.

1. Billie	**a.** Bette Davis in *In This Our Life*
2. Butch	**b.** Irene Dunne in *Life with Father*
3. George	**c.** Judy Holliday in *Born Yesterday*
4. Stanley	**d.** Thelma Ritter in *Pickup on South Street*
5. Charlie	**e.** Teresa Wright in *Shadow of a Doubt*
6. Frankie	**f.** Jane Russell in *Son of Paleface*
7. Petey	**g.** Julie Harris in *The Member of the Wedding*
8. Moe	**h.** Merle Oberon in *A Song to Remember*
9. Mike	**i.** Ida Lupino in *The Man I Love*
10. Vinnie	**j.** June Allyson in *The McConnell Story*

2. Match the equally surprising first name (or nickname) of a screen character to the actor who played him.

1. Hot Lips	**a.** Joseph Cotten in *The Third Man*
2. Connie	**b.** Arthur Kennedy in *Champion*
3. Clare	**c.** Raymond Massey in *The Fountainhead*
4. Candy	**d.** Clark Gable in *The Misfits*
5. Holly	**e.** John Ireland in *Red River*
6. Laurie	**f.** Clifton Webb in *Sitting Pretty*
7. Gail	**g.** Clark Gable in *Honky Tonk*
8. Cherry	**h.** Bob Hope in *Road to Rio*
9. Gay	**i.** Peter Sellers in *Lolita*
10. Lynn	**j.** Peter Lawford in *Little Women*

3. Match the title character to her last name.

1. *Laura*	**a.** Mundson
2. *Sabrina*	**b.** Clary
3. *Rebecca*	**c.** Hunt
4. *Gilda*	**d.** MacDuff
5. *Marnie*	**e.** De Winter
6. *Margie*	**f.** Johnson
7. *Lili*	**g.** Haze
8. *Desiree*	**h.** Fairchild
9. *Lolita*	**i.** Daurier
10. *Pinky*	**j.** Edgar

4. Match the title character to his first name.

1.	*Mr. Deeds Goes to Town*	**a.**	Peter
2.	*Mr. Smith Goes to Washington*	**b.**	Longfellow
3.	*Sullivan's Travels*	**c.**	Cosmo
4.	*Mister Roberts*	**d.**	Henry
5.	*Topper*	**e.**	John
6.	*Destry Rides Again*	**f.**	Sam
7.	*Dodsworth*	**g.**	Alvin
8.	*Frankenstein*	**h.**	Jefferson
9.	*Sergeant York*	**i.**	Tom
10.	*Captain Blood*	**j.**	Doug

5. Match the title character to the actress who played her.

1.	*Nora Prentiss*	**a.**	Jennifer Jones
2.	*Ruby Gentry*	**b.**	Jane Wyman
3.	*Evelyn Prentice*	**c.**	Ginger Rogers
4.	*Letty Lynton*	**d.**	Jean Simmons
5.	*Lucy Gallant*	**e.**	Ann Sheridan
6.	*Alice Adams*	**f.**	Joan Crawford
7.	*Hilda Crane*	**g.**	Myrna Loy
8.	*Ann Vickers*	**h.**	Irene Dunne
9.	*Roxie Hart*	**i.**	Miriam Hopkins
10.	*Becky Sharp*	**j.**	Katharine Hepburn

6. Match the title character to the actor who played him.

1.	*Cass Timberlane*	**a.**	Robert Taylor
2.	*Lucky Jordan*	**b.**	Gary Cooper
3.	*Sorrowful Jones*	**c.**	Fredric March
4.	*Will Penny*	**d.**	Alan Ladd
5.	*Peter Ibbetson*	**e.**	William Holden
6.	*Boots Malone*	**f.**	Bob Hope
7.	*Bulldog Drummond*	**g.**	Mickey Rooney
8.	*Anthony Adverse*	**h.**	Spencer Tracy
9.	*Quentin Durward*	**i.**	Ronald Colman
10.	*Killer McCoy*	**j.**	Charlton Heston

7. The title role is not always the starring role. Match the title character to the supporting actor who played him.

1.	*Gunga Din* (starring Cary Grant)	**a.**	Claude Rains
2.	*Julius Caesar* (starring Marlon Brando)	**b.**	Joseph Wiseman
3.	*The Wizard of Oz* (starring Judy Garland)	**c.**	Walter Slezak
4.	*Dr. No* (starring Sean Connery)	**d.**	Wayne Morris
5.	*The Pirate* (starring Gene Kelly)	**e.**	Louis Calhern
6.	*The Thin Man* (starring William Powell)	**f.**	Edward Ellis
		g.	Sam Jaffe
7.	*Topper* (starring Cary Grant)	**h.**	Dean Jagger
8.	*Kid Galahad* (starring Edward G. Robinson)	**i.**	Frank Morgan
9.	*Brigham Young* (starring Tyrone Power)	**j.**	Roland Young
10.	*Here Comes Mr. Jordan* (starring Robert Montgomery)		

8. Match the blissfully silly character name to the actress who played her.

1.	Trudy Kockenlocker	**a.**	Judy Holliday in *It Should Happen to You*
2.	Luisa Ginglebusher	**b.**	Barbara Stanwyck in *Ball of Fire*
3.	Muzzy Van Hossmere	**c.**	Margaret Sullavan in *The Good Fairy*
4.	Gladys Glover	**d.**	Ginger Rogers in *The Gay Divorcee*
5.	Zelda Zanders	**e.**	Carol Channing in *Thoroughly Modern Millie*
6.	Sugarpuss O'Shea	**f.**	Betty Garrett in *On the Town*
7.	Phoebe Frost	**g.**	Rita Moreno in *Singin' in the Rain*
8.	Mimi Glossop	**h.**	Betty Hutton in *The Miracle of Morgan's Creek*
9.	Pola Debevoise	**i.**	Jean Arthur in *A Foreign Affair*
10.	Brunhilde Esterhazy	**j.**	Marilyn Monroe in *How to Marry a Millionaire*

9. Match the swell-egant character name to the actor who played him. Don't you wish you had a name like one of these?

1.	C. K. Dexter Haven	**a.**	Zachary Scott in *Mildred Pierce*
2.	Waldo Lydecker	**b.**	Joe E. Brown in *Some Like It Hot*
3.	Monte Beragon	**c.**	Robert Walker in *Strangers on a Train*
4.	Addison DeWitt	**d.**	Clifton Webb in *Laura*
5.	Bruno Anthony	**e.**	Cary Grant in *An Affair to Remember*
6.	J. J. Hunsecker	**f.**	George Sanders in *All About Eve*
7.	Osgood Fielding III	**g.**	Vincent Price in *Laura*
8.	Shelby Carpenter	**h.**	Humphrey Bogart in *Sabrina*
9.	Nickie Ferrante	**i.**	Cary Grant in *The Philadelphia Story*
10.	Linus Larrabee	**j.**	Burt Lancaster in *Sweet Smell of Success*

10. Match the "Hitchcock blonde" character to the actress who played her.

1. Charlotte Inwood
2. Margot Wendice
3. Gay Keane
4. Jo McKenna
5. Marion Crane
6. Judy Barton
7. Lisa Fremont

8. Eve Kendall
9. Melanie Daniels
10. Frances Stevens

a. Grace Kelly in *Dial M for Murder*
b. Grace Kelly in *Rear Window*
c. Grace Kelly in *To Catch a Thief*
d. Janet Leigh in *Psycho*
e. Tippi Hedren in *The Birds*
f. Marlene Dietrich in *Stage Fright*
g. Eva Marie Saint in *North by Northwest*
h. Ann Todd in *The Paradine Case*
i. Kim Novak in *Vertigo*
j. Doris Day in *The Man Who Knew Too Much*

11. Match the western character to the actor who played him.

1. Waco Johnny Dean
2. Johnny Ringo
3. Jimmy Ringo
4. The Ringo Kid
5. The Dancin' Kid
6. Billy the Kid
7. Kid Shelleen
8. Lewt McCanles

9. Ethan Edwards

10. Will Kane

a. John Wayne in *Stagecoach*
b. Gregory Peck in *Duel in the Sun*
c. Dan Duryea in *Winchester '73*
d. Gregory Peck in *The Gunfighter*
e. Gary Cooper in *High Noon*
f. Scott Brady in *Johnny Guitar*
g. John Wayne in *The Searchers*
h. John Ireland in *Gunfight at the O.K. Corral*
i. Paul Newman in *The Left-Handed Gun*
j. Lee Marvin in *Cat Ballou*

12. Match the Tennessee Williams character to the performer who played him/her on the screen. Then name the film.

1. Laura Wingfield   **a.** Vivien Leigh
2. Catherine Holly   **b.** Ava Gardner
3. Carol Cutrere   **c.** Anna Magnani
4. Karen Stone   **d.** Jane Wyman
5. Lady Torrance   **e.** Geraldine Page
6. Hannah Jelkes   **f.** Joanne Woodward
7. Maxine Faulk   **g.** Noël Coward
8. Heavenly Finley   **h.** Elizabeth Taylor
9. Alexandra Del Lago   **i.** Shirley Knight
10. The Witch of Capri   **j.** Deborah Kerr

13. Match the "Johnny" character to the actor who played him.

1. Johnny Friendly   **a.** Sterling Hayden in *Johnny Guitar*
2. Johnnie Gray   **b.** Cary Grant in *Suspicion*
3. Johnnie Aysgarth   **c.** Edward G. Robinson in *Key Largo*
4. Johnny Case   **d.** Don Murray in *A Hatful of Rain*
5. Johnny Farrell   **e.** Lee J. Cobb in *On the Waterfront*
6. Johnny Logan   **f.** James Mason in *Odd Man Out*
7. Johnny Pope   **g.** Glenn Ford in *Gilda*
8. Johnny Nolan   **h.** Buster Keaton in *The General*
9. Johnny Rocco   **i.** James Dunn in *A Tree Grows in Brooklyn*
10. Johnny McQueen   **j.** Cary Grant in *Holiday*

14. Match the real person to the actress who played her on the screen (in the year listed by her name). Name the films too.

1. Emily Brontë
2. Dolly Madison
3. Sheilah Graham
4. Barbara Graham
5. Elizabeth I
6. Elizabeth Kenny
7. Elizabeth Barrett Browning
8. Billie Burke
9. Calamity Jane
10. Eleanor Roosevelt

a. Susan Hayward (1958)
b. Deborah Kerr (1959)
c. Jean Arthur (1936)
d. Greer Garson (1960)
e. Ida Lupino (1946)
f. Myrna Loy (1936)
g. Jean Simmons (1953)
h. Jennifer Jones (1957)
i. Ginger Rogers (1946)
j. Rosalind Russell (1946)

15. Match the real person to the actor who played him on the screen (in the year listed by his name). Name the films too.

1. Andrew Jackson
2. Rembrandt
3. Thomas Alva Edison
4. Dr. Paul Ehrlich
5. Benito Juárez
6. Pancho Villa
7. Charles Lindbergh
8. Mark Twain
9. Ernie Pyle
10. Aaron Burr

a. Paul Muni (1939)
b. Fredric March (1944)
c. Wallace Beery (1934)
d. Charles Laughton (1936)
e. Edward G. Robinson (1940)
f. David Niven (1946)
g. Lionel Barrymore (1936)
h. James Stewart (1957)
i. Burgess Meredith (1945)
j. Spencer Tracy (1940)

16. Some characters are talked about a great deal without actually appearing. They may be seen in photographs or even heard on the soundtrack. Some of them are just plain dead. Match each character to the film in which he/she is important to the story but remains unseen.

1. Claude Daigle	**a.**	*Laura*
2. Tina Mara	**b.**	*A Letter to Three Wives*
3. Stephen Haines	**c.**	*The King and I*
4. Addie Ross	**d.**	*The Philadelphia Story*
5. Tim Hilton	**e.**	*A Streetcar Named Desire*
6. Diane Redfern	**f.**	*The Maltese Falcon* (1941)
7. Shep Huntleigh	**g.**	*The Women*
8. Tom Leonowens	**h.**	*The Bad Seed*
9. Floyd Thursby	**i.**	*The Miracle of Morgan's Creek*
10. Private Ratzkiwatzki	**j.**	*Since You Went Away*

17. Match the clownish character name to the man who played him.

1. Rufus T. Firefly   **a.** W. C. Fields in *My Little Chickadee*

2. Julius Kelp   **b.** Red Skelton in *Neptune's Daughter*

3. Jack Spratt   **c.** Sterling Hayden in *Dr. Strangelove*

4. Egbert Sousé   **d.** Groucho Marx in *A Night at the Opera*

5. Jack D. Ripper   **e.** Jerry Lewis in *The Nutty Professor*

6. Buzzy Bellew   **f.** Charlie Chaplin in *The Great Dictator*

7. Cuthbert J. Twillie   **g.** Jerry Lewis in *Scared Stiff*

8. Adenoid Hynkel   **h.** Groucho Marx in *Duck Soup*

9. Otis P. Driftwood   **i.** Danny Kaye in *Wonder Man*

10. Myron Myron Mertz   **j.** W. C. Fields in *The Bank Dick*

18. Sometimes a character is known by two different names over the course of one movie. Whatever the reason (career move, amnesia, undercover work, etc.), it usually leads to complications. Match the double-named character to the film in which he/she appears.

1. Anthony Edwardes/   **a.** *Lady for a Day*
   John Ballantine

2. Ethel Whitehead/   **b.** *Twentieth Century*
   Lorna Hansen Forbes

3. Joe Pendleton/   **c.** *Midnight*
   Bruce Farnsworth

4. Mildred Plotka/   **d.** *The Damned Don't Cry*
   Lily Garland

5. Brad Allen/   **e.** *Spellbound*
   Rex Stetson

6. Eve Peabody/   **f.** *Mr. Deeds Goes to Town*
   Baroness Czerny

7. Apple Annie/   **g.** *The Palm Beach Story*
   Mrs. E. Worthington
   Manville

8. Tom Jeffers/   **h.** *Pillow Talk*
   Captain McGloo

9. Babe Bennett/   **i.** *Here Comes Mr. Jordan*
   Mary Dawson

10. Johnny Jones/   **j.** *Foreign Correspondent*
    Huntley Haverstock

19. It's always a jolt when there is a character in an old movie with a name that would become famous in the years since the film was made. Match each character to the actor who played him.

1. Gig Young
2. Steve Martin
3. Oliver Stone
4. Oliver Reed
5. Chris Farley
6. John Kennedy
7. Harry Morgan
8. Christopher Cross
9. Chris Jorgenson
10. Larry Flint

a. Edward G. Robinson in *Scarlet Street*
b. Cesar Romero in *The Thin Man*
c. William Demarest in *The Jolson Story*
d. George Nader in *The Female Animal*
e. Humphrey Bogart in *To Have and Have Not*
f. Kent Smith in *Cat People*
g. Gig Young in *The Gay Sisters*
h. Walter Connolly in *Nothing Sacred*
i. Paul Newman in *What a Way to Go!*
j. Dick Powell in *The Tall Target*

20. You remember the face, you remember the scenes, but do you remember the performer's name? Pick the performer on the right who played each of the unforgettable roles on the left.

1. "Teddy Roosevelt" Brewster in *Arsenic and Old Lace*

   a. John Alexander; **b.** Jerry Colonna; **c.** Walter Abel; **d.** Allyn Joslyn

2. Lina Lamont in *Singin' in the Rain*

   a. Jan Sterling; **b.** Barbara Nichols; **c.** Jean Hagen; **d.** Jane Greer

3. Countess De Lave in *The Women*

   a. Laura Hope Crews; **b.** Billie Burke; **c.** Constance Bennett; **d.** Mary Boland

4. Maggie Prescott in *Funny Face*

   a. Dolores Gray; **b.** Kay Thompson; **c.** Nina Foch; **d.** Janis Paige

5. Mrs. Van Hopper in *Rebecca*

   a. Ilka Chase; **b.** Florence Bates; **c.** Lucile Watson; **d.** Constance Collier

6. Madame Defarge in *A Tale of Two Cities* (1936)

   a. Blanche Yurka; **b.** Alla Nazimova; **c.** Katina Paxinou; **d.** Maria Ouspenskaya

7. Jeffrey Cordova in *The Band Wagon*

   a. Georges Guetary; **b.** Hans Conried; **c.** Anton Walbrook; **d.** Jack Buchanan

8. Lady Catherine de Bourgh in *Pride and Prejudice*

   a. May Whitty; **b.** Marie Dressler; **c.** Edith Evans; **d.** Edna May Oliver

9. Vera Charles in *Auntie Mame*

   a. Kay Walsh; **b.** Coral Browne; **c.** Pamela Brown; **d.** Joan Greenwood

10. Belle Watling in *Gone With the Wind*

   a. Ina Claire; **b.** Osa Massen; **c.** Ona Munson; **d.** Claire Trevor

The cast of MGM's *Pride and Prejudice*

TWO

"Family Plot"

21. Match the actress to the film in which she played a mother.

1. Spring Byington	**a.** *Citizen Kane*	
2. Anne Revere	**b.** *Gone With the Wind*	
3. Beulah Bondi	**c.** *Mutiny on the Bounty* (1935)	
4. Agnes Moorehead	**d.** *White Heat*	
5. Jo Van Fleet	**e.** *Dead End*	
6. Margaret Wycherly	**f.** *Our Town*	
7. Barbara O'Neil	**g.** *My Man Godfrey* (1936)	
8. Marjorie Main	**h.** *A Place in the Sun*	
9. Alice Brady	**i.** *Kitty Foyle*	
10. Gladys Cooper	**j.** *I'll Cry Tomorrow*	

22. Match the actor to the film in which he played a father.

1.	Frank Morgan	a.	*Johnny Belinda*
2.	Donald Crisp	b.	*Pride and Prejudice*
3.	Thomas Mitchell	c.	*How Green Was My Valley*
4.	Charles Bickford	d.	*My Darling Clementine*
5.	Samuel S. Hinds	e.	*The Mortal Storm*
6.	Edmund Gwenn	f.	*It Happened One Night*
7.	Claude Rains	g.	*The Furies*
8.	Walter Connolly	h.	*Gone With the Wind*
9.	Walter Huston	i.	*Kings Row*
10.	Walter Brennan	j.	*It's a Wonderful Life*

23. Match the child actress to the film in which she appeared.

1.	Natalie Wood	a.	*The Keys of the Kingdom*
2.	Elizabeth Taylor	b.	*The Bad Seed*
3.	Margaret O'Brien	c.	*The White Cliffs of Dover*
4.	Peggy Ann Garner	d.	*Gone With the Wind*
5.	Bonita Granville	e.	*These Three*
6.	Patty McCormack	f.	*The Philadelphia Story*
7.	Cammie King	g.	*To Kill a Mockingbird*
8.	Patty Duke	h.	*The Ghost and Mrs. Muir*
9.	Mary Badham	i.	*The Goddess*
10.	Virginia Weidler	j.	*Our Vines Have Tender Grapes*

24. Match the child actor to the film in which he appeared.

1.	Freddie Bartholomew	a.	*Gentleman's Agreement*
2.	Scotty Beckett	b.	*The Champ* (1931)
3.	Jackie Cooper	c.	*National Velvet*
4.	Darryl Hickman	d.	*Beau Geste* (1939)
5.	Dean Stockwell	e.	*Anna Karenina* (1935)
6.	Donald O'Connor	f.	*Tarzan Finds a Son!*
7.	Roddy McDowall	g.	*The Yearling*
8.	Johnny Sheffield	h.	*Kings Row*
9.	Jackie "Butch" Jenkins	i.	*The Pied Piper*
10.	Claude Jarman, Jr.	j.	*Leave Her to Heaven*

25. Match the actress to the aunt she played on the screen (in the year listed by her name). How about naming the films too?

1.	Agnes Moorehead (1942)	a.	Aunt Abby
2.	Fay Bainter (1938)	b.	Aunt March
3.	Clara Blandick (1939)	c.	Aunt Lavinia
4.	Josephine Hull (1944)	d.	Aunt Fanny
5.	Joan Blondell (1945)	e.	Aunt Birdie
6.	Miriam Hopkins (1949)	f.	Aunt Pittypat
7.	Patricia Collinge (1941)	g.	Aunt Belle
8.	Edna May Oliver (1933)	h.	Aunt Sissy
9.	Laura Hope Crews (1939)	i.	Aunt Eller
10.	Charlotte Greenwood (1955)	j.	Aunt Em

26. Match the fictional family to the film that tells their story.

1. The Stephensons	**a.** *Seven Brides for Seven Brothers*
2. The Morgans	**b.** *Meet Me in St. Louis*
3. The Pontipees	**c.** *Shane*
4. The Benedicts	**d.** *National Velvet*
5. The Sycamores	**e.** *The Best Years of Our Lives*
6. The Starretts	**f.** *Giant*
7. The Baxters	**g.** *How Green Was My Valley*
8. The Browns	**h.** *My Man Godfrey*
9. The Bullocks	**i.** *The Yearling*
10. The Smiths	**j.** *You Can't Take It With You*

27. Match the first names of two performers with the same last name to the film in which they both appeared. Some of the pairs are related and some are not.

1. Kirk and Paul	**a.** *Tea and Sympathy*
2. James and Paul	**b.** *Night Flight*
3. James and Jeanne	**c.** *The V.I.P.s*
4. Hayley and John	**d.** *Carbine Williams*
5. Deborah and John	**e.** *The Chalk Garden*
6. Lionel and John	**f.** *The Time of Your Life*
7. Elizabeth and Robert	**g.** *The Proud Rebel*
8. Elizabeth and Rod	**h.** *Conspirator*
9. Alan and David	**i.** *A Letter to Three Wives*
10. Bette and James	**j.** *Winter Meeting*

28. Match the performer to the film in which he/she is related to Shirley Temple.

1. Gary Cooper
   (her father)
2. Joel McCrea
   (her father)
3. Henry Fonda
   (her father)
4. Ginger Rogers
   (her cousin)
5. Myrna Loy
   (her sister)
6. Lionel Barrymore
   (her grandfather)
7. Jean Hersholt
   (her grandfather)
8. C. Aubrey Smith
   (her grandfather)
9. Claire Trevor
   (her mother)
10. Claudette Colbert
   (her mother)

a. *Baby Take a Bow*

b. *Since You Went Away*

c. *Now and Forever*

d. *Fort Apache*

e. *Wee Willie Winkie*

f. *The Little Colonel*

g. *I'll Be Seeing You*

h. *Heidi*

i. *Our Little Girl*

j. *The Bachelor and the Bobby-Soxer*

29. Match the performer to the film in which he/she is related to Judy Garland.

1.	Gloria DeHaven (her sister)	**a.** *The Pirate*
2.	Charley Grapewin (her uncle)	**b.** *Everybody Sing*
3.	Gladys Cooper (her aunt)	**c.** *Meet Me in St. Louis*
4.	Robert Walker (her husband)	**d.** *The Clock*
5.	Stuart Erwin (her brother)	**e.** *In the Good Old Summertime*
6.	Billie Burke (her mother)	**f.** *Summer Stock*
7.	George Murphy (her father)	**g.** *Pigskin Parade*
8.	Liza Minnelli (her daughter)	**h.** *Girl Crazy*
9.	Nancy Walker (her cousin)	**i.** *The Wizard of Oz*
10.	Leon Ames (her father)	**j.** *Little Nellie Kelly*

30. Match the performer to the film in which he/she is related to Elizabeth Taylor.

1. Donald Crisp (her father)	**a.** *Little Women*
2. Carroll Baker (her daughter)	**b.** *The Last Time I Saw Paris*
3. Donna Reed (her sister)	**c.** *Suddenly, Last Summer*
4. Janet Leigh (her sister)	**d.** *Butterfield 8*
5. Jack Carson (her brother-in-law)	**e.** *A Place in the Sun*
6. Mildred Dunnock (her mother)	**f.** *National Velvet*
7. Billie Burke (her mother-in-law)	**g.** *Lassie Come Home*
8. Mercedes McCambridge (her mother)	**h.** *Cat on a Hot Tin Roof*
9. Shepperd Strudwick (her father)	**i.** *Giant*
10. Nigel Bruce (her grandfather)	**j.** *Father's Little Dividend*

31. Sisters Olivia de Havilland and Joan Fontaine worked with some of the same actors. The first film in each pair features Fontaine and the second features de Havilland. Match the pair of films to the actor who appeared in both of them.

1. *The Constant Nymph/* **a.** Joseph Cotten
   Hold Back the Dawn

2. *September Affair/* **b.** Mark Stevens
   Hush . . . Hush,
   Sweet Charlotte

3. *Something to Live For/* **c.** John Lund
   The Well-Groomed
   Bride

4. *Darling, How* **d.** Ray Milland
   Could You!/
   To Each His Own

5. *From This Day* **e.** Charles Boyer
   Forward/
   The Snake Pit

6. *Frenchman's Creek/* **f.** Rossano Brazzi
   Captain Blood

7. *The Affairs of Susan/* **g.** Patric Knowles
   In This Our Life

8. *Serenade/* **h.** George Brent
   The Private Lives of
   Elizabeth and Essex

9. *A Certain Smile/* **i.** Vincent Price
   Light in the Piazza

10. *Ivy/* **j.** Basil Rathbone
    The Charge of the
    Light Brigade

32. Henry and Jane Fonda may have been from different generations, but they still managed to work with some of the same performers. The first film in each pair features Henry and the second features Jane. Match each pair of films to the performer who appeared in both of them. Some of these films are all-star affairs and the Fondas don't always share actual screen time with each performer.

1. *The Best Man/*
   Sunday in New York

2. *Once Upon a Time*
   in the West/
   Any Wednesday

3. *Mister Roberts/*
   The China Syndrome

4. *Tales of Manhattan/*
   Barefoot in the Park

5. *You Belong to Me/*
   Walk on the Wild
   Side

6. *Advise and Consent/*
   Hurry Sundown

7. *Ash Wednesday/*
   The Blue Bird

8. *The Tin Star/*
   Tall Story

9. *Twelve Angry Men/*
   The Chase

10. *Sex and the Single*
    Girl/
    Cat Ballou

a. Jack Lemmon

b. Elizabeth Taylor

c. Barbara Stanwyck

d. Anthony Perkins

e. Stubby Kaye

f. Jason Robards

g. Cliff Robertson

h. Charles Boyer

i. E. G. Marshall

j. Burgess Meredith

Laurence Olivier and Joan Fontaine in *Rebecca*

THREE

"This Land Is Mine"

33. Match the actor to the king he played in a film (in the year listed by his name). Grab some extra credit and name the films.

1. Claude Rains (1938)
2. Rex Harrison (1946)
3. Wallace Beery (1922)
4. George Sanders (1947 and 1955)
5. Frank Morgan (1948)
6. Basil Rathbone (1939)
7. Mel Ferrer (1953)
8. Robert Morley (1938)
9. Peter O'Toole (1964 and 1968)
10. Laurence Olivier (1944)

a. Charles II
b. Richard the Lionhearted
c. Louis XVI
d. Richard III
e. King of Siam
f. Henry II
g. Louis XIII
h. Henry V
i. King John
j. King Arthur

34. Match the actress to the queen she played in a film (in the year listed by her name). And while you're at it, name the films, too.

1.	Deborah Kerr (1953)	**a.**	Queen Herodias
2.	Viveca Lindfors (1948)	**b.**	Queen Elizabeth I
3.	Katharine Hepburn (1968)	**c.**	Queen Anne of France
4.	Judith Anderson (1953)	**d.**	Catherine Parr
5.	Ethel Barrymore (1932)	**e.**	Empress Alexandra
6.	Flora Robson (1937 and 1940)	**f.**	Anne Boleyn
7.	Ava Gardner (1953)	**g.**	Queen Margaret of Spain
8.	Merle Oberon (1933)	**h.**	Queen Victoria
9.	Irene Dunne (1950)	**i.**	Eleanor of Aquitaine
10.	Angela Lansbury (1948)	**j.**	Queen Guinevere

35. Match the piece of real estate to the film in which it appears.

1. Spanish Bit	**a.** *Gone With the Wind*
2. Twelve Oaks	**b.** *Duel in the Sun*
3. Reata	**c.** *Citizen Kane*
4. Peckerwood	**d.** *The Ghost and Mrs. Muir*
5. Gull Cottage	**e.** *Spellbound*
6. Xanadu	**f.** *Leave Her to Heaven*
7. Cascade	**g.** *Giant*
8. Green Manors	**h.** *Rebecca*
9. Back of the Moon	**i.** *Now, Voyager*
10. Manderley	**j.** *Auntie Mame*

36. Match the first name (or nickname) of a screen character to the performer who played it.

1. Kansas	**a.** Betty Hutton in *Incendiary Blonde*
2. Dallas	**b.** Shirley Temple in *Fort Apache*
3. Texas	**c.** Olivia de Havilland in *The Snake Pit*
4. Georgia	**d.** Ricky Nelson in *Rio Bravo*
5. Virginia	**e.** Glenda Farrell in *Lady for a Day*
6. Nevada	**f.** Sonny Tufts in *So Proudly We Hail!*
7. Missouri	**g.** Dorothy Lamour in *Chad Hanna*
8. Colorado	**h.** Lana Turner in *The Bad and the Beautiful*
9. Albany	**i.** Alan Ladd in *The Carpetbaggers*
10. Philadelphia	**j.** Claire Trevor in *Stagecoach*

37. Match the film to the city in which it is primarily set.

1.	*Double Indemnity*	a.	San Francisco
2.	*The Third Man*	b.	Berlin
3.	*The Shop Around the Corner*	c.	Los Angeles
4.	*Born Yesterday*	d.	New York
5.	*Vertigo*	e.	Vienna
6.	*The Heiress*	f.	Washington, D.C.
7.	*Ninotchka*	g.	London
8.	*Notorious*	h.	Rio de Janeiro
9.	*Gaslight*	i.	Budapest
10.	*One, Two, Three*	j.	Paris

38. Match the film to the country in which it is primarily set.

1.	*Johnny Belinda*	a.	China
2.	*The Keys of the Kingdom*	b.	Sweden
3.	*On the Beach*	c.	U.S.A.
4.	*Gilda*	d.	Spain
5.	*I Remember Mama*	e.	Australia
6.	*Hold Back the Dawn*	f.	France
7.	*All This, and Heaven Too*	g.	Turkey
8.	*Queen Christina*	h.	Argentina
9.	*America, America*	i.	Mexico
10.	*For Whom the Bell Tolls*	j.	Canada

39. Match the film about World War II (or the years leading up to it) to the country in which it is primarily set.

1.	*The Diary of Anne Frank*	**a.**	Burma
2.	*To Be or Not to Be*	**b.**	Germany
3.	*The Seventh Cross*	**c.**	U.S.A.
4.	*Mrs. Miniver*	**d.**	Italy
5.	*The Hasty Heart*	**e.**	Japan
6.	*A Walk in the Sun*	**f.**	Holland
7.	*Five Fingers*	**g.**	England
8.	*The North Star*	**h.**	Russia
9.	*The Purple Heart*	**i.**	Poland
10.	*Watch on the Rhine*	**j.**	Turkey

40. Many actors put movie stardom on hold to serve in World War II. When they returned, the Hollywood publicity machine made much of their comeback vehicles. Match the actor to his first post-WWII film. As you can see, some fared far better than others.

1. Robert Taylor	**a.**	*The Razor's Edge*
2. Clark Gable	**b.**	*The Strange Love of Martha Ivers*
3. Van Heflin	**c.**	*The Dark Mirror*
4. Robert Montgomery	**d.**	*Adventure*
5. William Holden	**e.**	*Sinbad the Sailor*
6. Tyrone Power	**f.**	*They Were Expendable*
7. Douglas Fairbanks, Jr.	**g.**	*Wild Harvest*
8. Victor Mature	**h.**	*Blaze of Noon*
9. Robert Preston	**i.**	*Undercurrent*
10. Lew Ayres	**j.**	*My Darling Clementine*

41. Match the exotic film title to one of its stars.

1. *Istanbul*	**a.**	Alan Ladd
2. *Macao*	**b.**	Maria Montez
3. *Sudan*	**c.**	Tyrone Power
4. *Honolulu*	**d.**	Jeanette MacDonald
5. *Cairo*	**e.**	Errol Flynn
6. *Calcutta*	**f.**	Maureen O'Hara
7. *Suez*	**g.**	Charles Boyer
8. *Malaya*	**h.**	Jane Russell
9. *Bagdad*	**i.**	Spencer Tracy
10. *Algiers*	**j.**	Eleanor Powell

42. Match the performer to his/her place of birth.

1.	Errol Flynn	**a.**	Japan
2.	Raymond Massey	**b.**	U.S.A.
3.	Vivien Leigh	**c.**	England
4.	Olivia de Havilland	**d.**	Canada
5.	Louis Hayward	**e.**	Ireland
6.	Deborah Kerr	**f.**	Tasmania
7.	Bob Hope	**g.**	Belgium
8.	Greer Garson	**h.**	South Africa
9.	Audrey Hepburn	**i.**	India
10.	Fred Astaire	**j.**	Scotland

Alan Ladd in *This Gun for Hire*

FOUR

"Career"

43. Match the star to the film in which he/she made an early (and very brief) screen appearance.

1.	Audrey Hepburn	a.	*Criss Cross*
2.	Alan Ladd	b.	*Top Hat*
3.	Tony Curtis	c.	*Since You Went Away*
4.	James Dean	d.	*Has Anybody Seen My Gal*
5.	David Niven	e.	*Citizen Kane*
6.	Gary Cooper	f.	*Gentleman's Agreement*
7.	Myrna Loy	g.	*The Lavender Hill Mob*
8.	Lucille Ball	h.	*Rose Marie* (1936)
9.	Dorothy Dandridge	i.	*Wings*
10.	Gene Nelson	j.	*The Jazz Singer* (1927)

44. Match the star to the film from a popular series in which he/she appeared.

1. Jeanette MacDonald	**a.**	*Andy Hardy's Double Life*
2. John Barrymore	**b.**	*Blondie on a Budget*
3. Esther Williams	**c.**	*Maisie Goes to Reno*
4. Lana Turner	**d.**	*Calling Dr. Kildare*
5. Anthony Quinn	**e.**	*The Sun Comes Up* (Lassie film)
6. Rita Hayworth	**f.**	*The Adventures of Sherlock Holmes*
7. Ava Gardner	**g.**	*Charlie Chan in London*
8. James Stewart	**h.**	*Bulldog Drummond's Revenge*
9. Ida Lupino	**i.**	*After the Thin Man*
10. Ray Milland	**j.**	*Road to Morocco*

45. Match the star to the famous film in which he/she had a supporting role.

1. Humphrey Bogart	**a.**	*The Best Years of Our Lives*
2. Susan Hayward	**b.**	*Winchester '73*
3. Rock Hudson	**c.**	*Life with Father*
4. Joan Fontaine	**d.**	*Out of the Past*
5. Mickey Rooney	**e.**	*Captains Courageous*
6. Virginia Mayo	**f.**	*Gunga Din*
7. Elizabeth Taylor	**g.**	*Beau Geste* (1939)
8. Natalie Wood	**h.**	*The Ox-Bow Incident*
9. Kirk Douglas	**i.**	*The Searchers*
10. Anthony Quinn	**j.**	*Dark Victory*

46. Match the not-so-famous performer to the very famous film in which he/she starred or at least played a very important role.

1. Barbara Parkins	**a.** *Guess Who's Coming to Dinner*	
2. Tom Tryon	**b.** *Peyton Place*	
3. Dorothy Comingore	**c.** *East of Eden*	
4. Richard Davalos	**d.** *King Kong* (1933)	
5. Millie Perkins	**e.** *Citizen Kane*	
6. Virginia Cherrill	**f.** *Valley of the Dolls*	
7. Katharine Houghton	**g.** *The Broadway Melody*	
8. Charles King	**h.** *City Lights*	
9. Robert Armstrong	**i.** *The Cardinal*	
10. Lee Philips	**j.** *The Diary of Anne Frank*	

47. Following each famous film, I have listed the actor most associated with it. However, these actors were not necessarily the stars of these films. Match each film to the actor who is the top-billed male in its opening credits.

1. *The Bridge on the River Kwai* —Alec Guinness   **a.** Joel McCrea

2. *Flying Down to Rio* —Fred Astaire   **b.** Robert Young

3. *This Gun for Hire* —Alan Ladd   **c.** George Sanders

4. *Frankenstein* —Boris Karloff   **d.** William Holden

5. *Dead End*— Humphrey Bogart   **e.** Colin Clive

6. *Kind Hearts and Coronets* —Alec Guinness   **f.** Claude Rains

7. *Crossfire* —Robert Ryan   **g.** Robert Preston

8. *Miracle on 34th Street*— Edmund Gwenn   **h.** Dennis Price

9. *Four Daughters* —John Garfield   **i.** Gene Raymond

10. *The Picture of Dorian Gray*— Hurd Hatfield   **j.** John Payne

48. Hollywood was always looking for the next Greta Garbo or Marlene Dietrich. Sometimes they found one (Ingrid Bergman), but most often they didn't. Match the European actress to one of the films that failed to make her a Hollywood star.

1.	Elissa Landi	**a.**	*The Buccaneer* (1938)
2.	Bella Darvi	**b.**	*Sirocco*
3.	Franciska Gaal	**c.**	*The Paradine Case*
4.	Anna Sten	**d.**	*The Egyptian*
5.	Signe Hasso	**e.**	*The Sign of the Cross*
6.	Alida Valli	**f.**	*The Snows of Kilimanjaro*
7.	Mai Zetterling	**g.**	*The House on 92nd Street*
8.	Cornell Borchers	**h.**	*The Big Lift*
9.	Marta Toren	**i.**	*The Wedding Night*
10.	Hildegarde Neff	**j.**	*Knock on Wood*

49. Match the actor to the role that made him a star. Then name the film.

1.	James Cagney	**a.**	Tommy Udo
2.	Kirk Douglas	**b.**	Joe Bonaparte
3.	John Garfield	**c.**	Cal Trask
4.	Alan Ladd	**d.**	Mickey Borden
5.	William Holden	**e.**	Roy Earle
6.	Burt Lancaster	**f.**	Bud Stamper
7.	Humphrey Bogart	**g.**	The Swede
8.	Richard Widmark	**h.**	Tom Powers
9.	James Dean	**i.**	Raven
10.	Warren Beatty	**j.**	Midge Kelly

50. Match the actress to the role that made her a star. Then name the film.

1.	Lauren Bacall	**a.**	Marie Browning
2.	Jane Russell	**b.**	Ulah
3.	Kim Novak	**c.**	Kitty Collins
4.	Ava Gardner	**d.**	Lady Lou
5.	Greer Garson	**e.**	Anita Hoffman
6.	Rita Hayworth	**f.**	Katherine Chipping
7.	Dorothy Lamour	**g.**	Rose Loomis
8.	Ingrid Bergman	**h.**	Madge Owens
9.	Mae West	**i.**	Dona Sol
10.	Marilyn Monroe	**j.**	Rio

51. Match the star to the horror film or thriller in which he/she appeared in the twilight of his/her screen career.

1.	Joan Crawford	**a.**	*The Day of the Triffids*
2.	Bette Davis	**b.**	*The Night Walker*
3.	Herbert Marshall	**c.**	*Trog*
4.	Dana Andrews	**d.**	*The Fly* (1958)
5.	Barbara Stanwyck	**e.**	*Die! Die! My Darling!*
6.	Howard Keel	**f.**	*Burnt Offerings*
7.	Joan Fontaine	**g.**	*Lady in a Cage*
8.	Tallulah Bankhead	**h.**	*The Devil's Own* (1967)
9.	Ray Milland	**i.**	*Curse of the Demon*
10.	Olivia de Havilland	**j.**	*The Thing with Two Heads*

52. Match the "Golden Age" performer to the fairly recent film in which he/she appeared.

1.	Sylvia Sidney	**a.**	*Hannah and Her Sisters*
2.	Gloria Grahame	**b.**	*Misery*
3.	Van Johnson	**c.**	*The Shawshank Redemption*
4.	Lloyd Nolan	**d.**	*Dangerous Liaisons*
5.	James Whitmore	**e.**	*Melvin and Howard*
6.	Mildred Natwick	**f.**	*The Age of Innocence*
7.	Dorothy Malone	**g.**	*Edward Scissorhands*
8.	Alexis Smith	**h.**	*The Purple Rose of Cairo*
9.	Lauren Bacall	**i.**	*Beetlejuice*
10.	Vincent Price	**j.**	*Basic Instinct*

53. Match the star to the year in which he/she died.

1.	John Garfield	**a.**	1937
2.	Montgomery Clift	**b.**	1942
3.	Carole Lombard	**c.**	1946
4.	Betty Grable	**d.**	1952
5.	Jean Harlow	**e.**	1957
6.	W. C. Fields	**f.**	1961
7.	Joan Crawford	**g.**	1966
8.	Gary Cooper	**h.**	1969
9.	Humphrey Bogart	**i.**	1973
10.	Judy Garland	**j.**	1977

Joan Crawford and Norma Shearer in *The Women*

"Who Was That Lady?"

Hint: Each star has 5 correct answers.

54. Greta Garbo or Lillian Gish?

1. Who won the first N.Y. Film Critics Award for Best Actress?
2. Who starred with Ronald Colman in *The White Sister*?
3. Who starred with John Gilbert in *La Bohème*?
4. Who was in a film directed by Charles Laughton?
5. Who starred in *Love* (a silent version of *Anna Karenina*)?
6. Who was in *Commandos Strike at Dawn* with Paul Muni?
7. Who starred with Herbert Marshall in *The Painted Veil*?
8. Who received an Oscar nomination for her first talkie?
9. Who received a 1954 honorary Oscar?
10. Who received a 1970 honorary Oscar?

55. Greer Garson or Norma Shearer?

1. Who played Elizabeth Barrett Browning?
2. Who played Jane Austen's Elizabeth Bennet?
3. Whose last MGM film was *Her Cardboard Lover*?
4. Who appeared in a Shakespeare film directed by George Cukor?
5. Who appeared in a Shakespeare film directed by Joseph L. Mankiewicz?
6. Who starred in a sequel to the movie that won her an Oscar?
7. Who starred with Robert Taylor in *Escape*?
8. Who received five consecutive Best Actress Oscar nominations?
9. Who starred as Amanda in *Private Lives*?
10. Who co-starred with Joan Crawford in *When Ladies Meet*?

56. Joan Crawford or Bette Davis?

1. Who became a star in the silent era?
2. Who played Mildred in a 1934 John Cromwell film?
3. Who starred in an Otto Preminger film with Henry Fonda?
4. Who starred in a 1948 comedy with Robert Montgomery?
5. Who sang and danced in *Thank Your Lucky Stars*?
6. Who won the 1945 Best Actress Oscar?
7. Who played *Sadie McKee* and *Harriet Craig*?
8. Who starred as one of *The Sisters* in 1938?
9. Whose first film was *Bad Sister*?
10. Who played a 1937 Gertrude Lawrence stage role in a 1940 film?

57. Jean Arthur or Carole Lombard?

1. Who got to choose between Melvyn Douglas and Fred Mac-Murray in *Too Many Husbands*?
2. Who got caught between Cary Grant and Kay Francis in *In Name Only*?
3. Who played a dedicated nurse in *Vigil in the Night*?
4. Who starred as *The Ex-Mrs. Bradford* with William Powell?
5. Who starred in a 1941 Alfred Hitchcock comedy?
6. Who starred with Edward G. Robinson in a 1935 John Ford comedy?
7. Who was stranded on an island with Bing Crosby in *We're Not Dressing*?
8. Who played James Stewart's bride in *Made for Each Other*?
9. Who starred with John Wayne in *A Lady Takes a Chance*?
10. Who starred with Charles Boyer in *History Is Made at Night*?

58. Ida Lupino or Barbara Stanwyck?

 1. Who was never nominated for a Best Actress Oscar?
 2. Who starred in *Gambling Lady* and *The Lady Gambles*?
 3. Who was one of *The Gay Sisters* in 1942?
 4. Who was the unhappy farm girl transformed by love in *Deep Valley*?
 5. Who starred with Errol Flynn in *Cry Wolf*?
 6. Who married Humphrey Bogart in *The Two Mrs. Carrolls*?
 7. Who sang and danced with Olivia de Havilland in *Thank Your Lucky Stars*?
 8. Who made two films with Clark Gable?
 9. Who was the superintendent of 1955's *Women's Prison*?
 10. Who starred in the murder melodrama *Ladies in Retirement*?

59. Alice Faye or Jeanette MacDonald?

 1. Who starred in the musical remake of *Smilin' Through*?
 2. Who was *The Girl of the Golden West*?
 3. Who made an early appearance with Spencer Tracy in *Now I'll Tell*?
 4. Who starred in a 1942 film of a Rodgers and Hart musical fantasy?
 5. Who starred in a 1940 film of a Noël Coward musical?
 6. Who played Belle in a film about an 1871 disaster?
 7. Who sang "This Year's Kisses" in *On the Avenue*?
 8. Who made an attempt at film noir in *Fallen Angel*?
 9. Who played Jane Powell's mother in *Three Daring Daughters*?
 10. Who made a comeback as the mother in the 1962 *State Fair*?

60. Olivia de Havilland or Joan Fontaine?

1. Who was one of *The Women*?
2. Who starred with Brian Aherne in *The Great Garrick*?
3. Who starred in a 1952 adaptation of a Daphne du Maurier novel?
4. Who starred as Charlotte Brontë in *Devotion*?
5. Who appeared in a film version of a Shakespeare comedy?
6. Who was directed by Ida Lupino in *The Bigamist*?
7. Who appeared with Myrna Loy in *The Ambassador's Daughter*?
8. Who starred in *Island in the Sun* with Harry Belafonte?
9. Who was one of Fred Astaire's dance partners?
10. Whose list of leading men includes both Bing Crosby and Mario Lanza?

61. Jane Wyman or Loretta Young?

1. Who played Mrs. Will Rogers in *The Story of Will Rogers*?
2. Who starred in a 1950 Alfred Hitchcock thriller?
3. Who starred in a 1946 Orson Welles thriller?
4. Who starred in the 1949 comedy *Mother Is a Freshman*?
5. Who played a deaf woman in *And Now Tomorrow*?
6. Who was Oscar-nominated for the tearjerker *The Blue Veil*?
7. Who played a blonde moll reformed by prison in *Because of You*?
8. Who starred with James Stewart in the comedy *Magic Town*?
9. Who made five films with David Niven?
10. Who played the female lead in a Billy Wilder Best Picture Oscar winner?

62. Ava Gardner or Lana Turner?

1. Who starred with Clark Gable four times?
2. Who starred in Joseph L. Mankiewicz's 1954 film about Hollywood?
3. Who starred in Vincente Minnelli's 1952 film about Hollywood?
4. Who starred in the 1955 remake of *The Rains Came*?
5. Who took Joan Crawford's role in a remake of *Grand Hotel*?
6. Who appeared briefly as a model in *Two Girls and a Sailor*?
7. Who was the first to receive a Best Actress Oscar nomination?
8. Who appeared with Mickey Rooney in *Love Finds Andy Hardy*?
9. Who was in *Ghosts on the Loose* with Bela Lugosi and The East Side Kids?
10. Who took Mary Martin's role in the film version of a 1943 Broadway musical?

63. Audrey Hepburn or Grace Kelly?

1. Who won an Oscar for playing a princess?
2. Who acted with Peter Finch in a Fred Zinnemann drama?
3. Who took Wendy Hiller's role in a remake of a Shaw comedy?
4. Who took Mary Astor's role in a remake of a sexy 1932 hit?
5. Who was paired with Gary Cooper in a Billy Wilder comedy?
6. Who starred with Stewart Granger in *Green Fire*?
7. Who sang an Oscar-nominated song in a 1956 MGM musical?
8. Who was Oscar-nominated in the Best Supporting Actress category?
9. Who was directed by William Wyler three times?
10. Who fell for Louis Jourdan in a 1956 romantic comedy?

Tyrone Power and Joan Blondell in *Nightmare Alley*

SIX

"The Player"

64. Match the actress to the film in which she played a secretary.

1.	Ellen Corby	**a.**	*Anatomy of a Murder*
2.	Lucille Ball	**b.**	*Gentleman's Agreement*
3.	Eve Arden	**c.**	*The Dark Corner*
4.	Lee Patrick	**d.**	*Sunrise at Campobello*
5.	Jean Hagen	**e.**	*The Apartment*
6.	Nina Foch	**f.**	*Sabrina* (1954)
7.	Thelma Ritter	**g.**	*Executive Suite*
8.	June Havoc	**h.**	*Wife vs. Secretary*
9.	Jean Harlow	**i.**	*The Maltese Falcon* (1941)
10.	Edie Adams	**j.**	*Daddy Long Legs* (1955)

65. Match the actor to the film in which he played an Asian character (not always convincingly).

1.	Walter Huston	a.	*A Majority of One*
2.	Ricardo Montalban	b.	*Breakfast at Tiffany's*
3.	Orson Welles	c.	*The Hatchet Man*
4.	Alec Guinness	d.	*Dragon Seed*
5.	Paul Muni	e.	*The Left Hand of God*
6.	Edward G. Robinson	f.	*Sayonara*
7.	Lee J. Cobb	g.	*The Inn of the Sixth Happiness*
8.	Mickey Rooney	h.	*The Black Rose*
9.	Marlon Brando	i.	*The Good Earth*
10.	Robert Donat	j.	*The Teahouse of the August Moon*

66. Match the "bad girl" to the film in which she was "bad."

1.	Gloria Grahame	a.	*The Killing*
2.	Peggy Cummins	b.	*Nightmare Alley*
3.	Jan Sterling	c.	*Sudden Fear*
4.	Helen Walker	d.	*Criss Cross*
5.	Marie Windsor	e.	*Dead Reckoning*
6.	Marilyn Maxwell	f.	*Female on the Beach*
7.	Lizabeth Scott	g.	*Out of the Past*
8.	Audrey Totter	h.	*Gun Crazy*
9.	Jane Greer	i.	*Champion*
10.	Yvonne De Carlo	j.	*Tension*

67. Match the actor to the film in which he played the man on the case (cop, detective, inspector . . . you get the idea).

1.	Glenn Ford	**a.**	*Shadow of a Doubt*
2.	Cornel Wilde	**b.**	*Dial M for Murder*
3.	Macdonald Carey	**c.**	*Murder, My Sweet*
4.	George Raft	**d.**	*Cry of the City*
5.	Barry Fitzgerald	**e.**	*The Big Combo*
6.	Ralph Meeker	**f.**	*I Confess*
7.	Karl Malden	**g.**	*The Naked City*
8.	John Williams	**h.**	*Kiss Me Deadly*
9.	Dick Powell	**i.**	*Black Widow* (1954)
10.	Victor Mature	**j.**	*The Big Heat*

68. Match the actress to the film in which she played a nun. No, Joan Collins is not a typo.

1.	Joan Collins	**a.**	*Green Dolphin Street*
2.	Peggy Wood	**b.**	*Black Narcissus*
3.	Edith Evans	**c.**	*Come to the Stable*
4.	Rosalind Russell	**d.**	*Portrait of Jennie*
5.	Gladys Cooper	**e.**	*The Singing Nun*
6.	Celeste Holm	**f.**	*The Trouble with Angels*
7.	Lillian Gish	**g.**	*The Nun's Story*
8.	Deborah Kerr	**h.**	*The Sound of Music*
9.	Greer Garson	**i.**	*The Song of Bernadette*
10.	Donna Reed	**j.**	*Sea Wife*

69. Match the actor to the film in which he played a character with what were once referred to as "homosexual tendencies."

1.	Martin Landau	**a.**	*Billy Budd*
2.	Robert Ryan	**b.**	*The Sergeant*
3.	Don Murray	**c.**	*Rope*
4.	Farley Granger	**d.**	*Inside Daisy Clover*
5.	Wendell Corey	**e.**	*Victim*
6.	Dirk Bogarde	**f.**	*North by Northwest*
7.	Rod Steiger	**g.**	*Ben-Hur* (1959)
8.	Robert Redford	**h.**	*Advise and Consent*
9.	Anthony Hopkins	**i.**	*The Lion in Winter*
10.	Stephen Boyd	**j.**	*Desert Fury*

70. Match the nonblond actress to the film for which she became a blonde.

1.	Anne Baxter	**a.**	*Forever Amber*
2.	Natalie Wood	**b.**	*The Silver Chalice*
3.	Gene Tierney	**c.**	*The Fuzzy Pink Nightgown*
4.	Jane Russell	**d.**	*Beat the Devil*
5.	Linda Darnell	**e.**	*The Diary of a Chambermaid* (1946)
6.	Mary Astor	**f.**	*I Confess*
7.	Shirley MacLaine	**g.**	*The Palm Beach Story*
8.	Jennifer Jones	**h.**	*The Lady from Shanghai*
9.	Rita Hayworth	**i.**	*A Bell for Adano*
10.	Paulette Goddard	**j.**	*Career*

71. Match the "angry young man" of the British film world to the film in which he starred (and vented his frustrations).

1.	Richard Burton	**a.**	*This Sporting Life*
2.	Laurence Harvey	**b.**	*Saturday Night and Sunday Morning*
3.	David Warner	**c.**	*If . . .*
4.	Alan Bates	**d.**	*Morgan!*
5.	Tom Courtenay	**e.**	*Room at the Top*
6.	Richard Harris	**f.**	*The L-Shaped Room*
7.	Tom Bell	**g.**	*A Kind of Loving*
8.	Albert Finney	**h.**	*Look Back in Anger*
9.	Malcolm McDowell	**i.**	*The Angry Silence*
10.	Richard Attenborough	**j.**	*The Loneliness of the Long Distance Runner*

72. Match the actress to the western in which she appeared.

1.	Virginia Mayo	**a.**	*The Naked Spur*
2.	Janet Leigh	**b.**	*Gunfight at the O.K. Corral*
3.	Carroll Baker	**c.**	*Pursued*
4.	Ann Sheridan	**d.**	*Colorado Territory*
5.	Susan Hayward	**e.**	*Winchester '73*
6.	Teresa Wright	**f.**	*Dodge City*
7.	Jean Arthur	**g.**	*Man Without a Star*
8.	Shelley Winters	**h.**	*Rawhide*
9.	Rhonda Fleming	**i.**	*The Big Country*
10.	Jeanne Crain	**j.**	*Arizona*

73. Match the performer to the film in which he/she was blind.

1.	Claude Rains	**a.**	*The Enchanted Cottage*
2.	Ida Lupino	**b.**	*Thunder in the East*
3.	Dana Andrews	**c.**	*Night Song*
4.	James Cagney	**d.**	*Pride of the Marines*
5.	Herbert Marshall	**e.**	*Mr. Skeffington*
6.	John Garfield	**f.**	*The Light That Failed*
7.	Van Johnson	**g.**	*Bright Victory*
8.	Ronald Colman	**h.**	*On Dangerous Ground*
9.	Deborah Kerr	**i.**	*23 Paces to Baker Street*
10.	Arthur Kennedy	**j.**	*City for Conquest*

74. In the years of the studio system, actresses played women with a surprising range of careers that went far beyond wives and mothers. Match the actress to her profession.

1.	Jean Arthur in *A Foreign Affair*	**a.**	congresswoman
2.	Claudette Colbert in *Private Worlds*	**b.**	general physician
3.	Katharine Hepburn in *Christopher Strong*	**c.**	engineering teacher and lecturer
4.	Bette Davis in *Ex-Lady*	**d.**	aviatrix
5.	Myrna Loy in *Belles on Their Toes*	**e.**	concert pianist
6.	Mary Astor in *The Great Lie*	**f.**	newspaper columnist
7.	Greer Garson in *Blossoms in the Dust*	**g.**	restaurant chain owner
8.	Barbara Stanwyck in *Meet John Doe*	**h.**	psychiatrist
9.	Joan Crawford in *Mildred Pierce*	**i.**	commercial artist
10.	Jennifer Jones in *Love Is a Many-Splendored Thing*	**j.**	children's rights activist

75. Match the performer to the film in which he/she had amnesia.

1.	Greta Garbo	a.	*Random Harvest*
2.	Boris Karloff	b.	*I Love You Again*
3.	Ingrid Bergman	c.	*Singapore*
4.	William Powell	d.	*Spellbound*
5.	Jennifer Jones	e.	*Libel*
6.	John Hodiak	f.	*Charlie Chan at the Opera*
7.	Ava Gardner	g.	*Love Letters*
8.	Ronald Colman	h.	*Anastasia*
9.	Dirk Bogarde	i.	*As You Desire Me*
10.	Gregory Peck	j.	*Somewhere in the Night*

76. Sagas of unwed mothers were a staple of what were once known as "women's pictures." Match the actress to the film in which she got pregnant without being married (or had done so in her past).

1.	Katharine Hepburn	a.	*To Each His Own*
2.	Margaret Sullavan	b.	*A Woman Rebels*
3.	Bette Davis	c.	*The Sin of Madelon Claudet*
4.	Olivia de Havilland	d.	*My Foolish Heart*
5.	Joan Fontaine	e.	*Only Yesterday*
6.	Helen Hayes	f.	*The Life of Vergie Winters*
7.	Lana Turner	g.	*The Old Maid*
8.	Susan Hayward	h.	*White Banners*
9.	Fay Bainter	i.	*Letter from an Unknown Woman*
10.	Ann Harding	j.	*Peyton Place*

77. Match the comedy star to the feature film in which he/she starred.

1.	Buster Keaton	a.	*The Patsy*
2.	Charlie Chaplin	b.	*The Party*
3.	Harold Lloyd	c.	*The Navigator*
4.	W. C. Fields	d.	*The Freshman*
5.	Mae West	e.	*The Circus*
6.	Groucho Marx	f.	*A Southern Yankee*
7.	Danny Kaye	g.	*It's a Gift*
8.	Red Skelton	h.	*Go West, Young Man*
9.	Jerry Lewis	i.	*Up in Arms*
10.	Peter Sellers	j.	*Copacabana*

78. Vivien Leigh's Scarlett O'Hara will forever be the "Southern belle" performance by which all others are measured. Match each actress to the film in which she did her own version of a flirtatious and/or headstrong magnolia blossom.

1.	Patricia Neal	a.	*Jezebel*
2.	Susan Hayward	b.	*Wells Fargo*
3.	Margaret Sullavan	c.	*Tap Roots*
4.	Bette Davis	d.	*Belle Starr*
5.	Arlene Dahl	e.	*So Red the Rose*
6.	Gene Tierney	f.	*Another Part of the Forest*
7.	Elizabeth Taylor	g.	*Bright Leaf*
8.	Frances Dee	h.	*Raintree County*
9.	Constance Towers	i.	*A Southern Yankee*
10.	Ann Blyth	j.	*The Horse Soldiers*

79. Match the performer to the film in which he/she played two roles (anything from twins to inexplicable lookalikes). I apologize for excluding Maria Montez's unforgettable work in *Cobra Woman.*

1. Douglas Fairbanks, Jr.	**a.** *The Prisoner of Zenda* (1937)
2. Sylvia Sidney	**b.** *Here Come the Waves*
3. Edward G. Robinson	**c.** *That Night in Rio*
4. Betty Hutton	**d.** *The Whole Town's Talking*
5. Danny Kaye	**e.** *The Black Room*
6. Olivia de Havilland	**f.** *A Stolen Life*
7. Boris Karloff	**g.** *The Corsican Brothers*
8. Ronald Colman	**h.** *On the Riviera*
9. Bette Davis	**i.** *Thirty-Day Princess*
10. Don Ameche	**j.** *The Dark Mirror*

Cary Grant and Katharine Hepburn in *Bringing Up Baby*

SEVEN

"The Winning Team"

80. Match the director to the actress he married.

1. William Wyler	**a.** Merle Oberon
2. Anatole Litvak	**b.** Veronica Lake
3. Alexander Korda	**c.** Rita Hayworth
4. Orson Welles	**d.** Ann Todd
5. John Huston	**e.** Margaret Sullavan
6. Andre de Toth	**f.** Gloria Grahame
7. Richard Brooks	**g.** Evelyn Keyes
8. David Lean	**h.** Miriam Hopkins
9. Nicholas Ray	**i.** Maureen O'Sullivan
10. John Farrow	**j.** Jean Simmons

81. Match the movie stars who were married to each other.

1. Lew Ayres	**a.** Madeleine Carroll
2. John Payne	**b.** Paulette Goddard
3. William Powell	**c.** Ginger Rogers
4. Sterling Hayden	**d.** Rita Hayworth
5. Mickey Rooney	**e.** Ida Lupino
6. Dick Haymes	**f.** Eleanor Powell
7. Glenn Ford	**g.** Gloria DeHaven
8. Louis Hayward	**h.** Alice Faye
9. Burgess Meredith	**i.** Carole Lombard
10. Tony Martin	**j.** Ava Gardner

82. Match the married couple to the film in which they appeared together (before or during the marriage).

1. Jean Simmons/ Stewart Granger	**a.** *This Is My Affair*
2. Anne Baxter/ John Hodiak	**b.** *Woman in Hiding*
3. Joan Crawford/ Franchot Tone	**c.** *Sunday Dinner for a Soldier*
4. Frances Dee/ Joel McCrea	**d.** *The Bride Wore Red*
5. Jessica Tandy/ Hume Cronyn	**e.** *Another Part of the Forest*
6. Florence Eldridge/ Fredric March	**f.** *The Green Years*
7. Barbara Stanwyck/ Robert Taylor	**g.** *Footsteps in the Fog*
8. Ida Lupino/ Howard Duff	**h.** *Brother Rat*
9. June Allyson/ Dick Powell	**i.** *The Silver Cord*
10. Jane Wyman/ Ronald Reagan	**j.** *The Reformer and the Redhead*

83. Match the screen team to one of their lesser-known movies.

<table>
<tr><td>1. Myrna Loy/
William Powell</td><td>a. Remains to Be Seen</td></tr>
<tr><td>2. Greer Garson/
Walter Pidgeon</td><td>b. Hold Your Man</td></tr>
<tr><td>3. Dorothy Lamour/
Bob Hope</td><td>c. Double Wedding</td></tr>
<tr><td>4. June Allyson/
Van Johnson</td><td>d. Scandal at Scourie</td></tr>
<tr><td>5. Judy Garland/
Mickey Rooney</td><td>e. Here Come the Co-Eds</td></tr>
<tr><td>6. Lauren Bacall/
Humphrey Bogart</td><td>f. The Kid from Brooklyn</td></tr>
<tr><td>7. Virginia Mayo/
Danny Kaye</td><td>g. Thoroughbreds Don't Cry</td></tr>
<tr><td>8. Veronica Lake/
Alan Ladd</td><td>h. Saigon</td></tr>
<tr><td>9. Jean Harlow/
Clark Gable</td><td>i. Dark Passage</td></tr>
<tr><td>10. Bud Abbott/
Lou Costello</td><td>j. Caught in the Draft</td></tr>
</table>

84. Match the screen team to the musical in which they co-starred.

1. Kathryn Grayson/   **a.** *Call Me Mister*
   Mario Lanza

2. Kathryn Grayson/   **b.** *One Hour With You*
   Howard Keel

3. Ruby Keeler/   **c.** *Shipmates Forever*
   Dick Powell

4. Jane Powell/   **d.** *Jupiter's Darling*
   Vic Damone

5. Vera-Ellen/   **e.** *Lovely to Look At*
   Fred Astaire

6. Betty Grable/   **f.** *Thrill of a Romance*
   Dan Dailey

7. Esther Williams/   **g.** *Rich, Young and Pretty*
   Van Johnson

8. Ginger Rogers/   **h.** *That Midnight Kiss*
   Fred Astaire

9. Esther Williams/   **i.** *The Belle of New York*
   Howard Keel

10. Jeanette MacDonald/   **j.** *Carefree*
   Maurice Chevalier

85. Match the actor and actress who appeared together in three films.

1. David Niven   **a.** Ava Gardner
2. Jack Lemmon   **b.** Ginger Rogers
3. Cary Grant   **c.** June Allyson
4. Leslie Howard   **d.** Ingrid Bergman
5. Charles Boyer   **e.** Myrna Loy
6. James Stewart   **f.** Jean Simmons
7. James Mason   **g.** Bette Davis
8. Tyrone Power   **h.** Anne Baxter
9. Charles Laughton   **i.** Kim Novak
10. Robert Mitchum   **j.** Maureen O'Hara

86. Match the screen team to the number of films they made together.

1. Doris Day/   **a.** 1
   Rock Hudson

2. Katharine Hepburn/   **b.** 2
   Spencer Tracy

3. Maria Montez/   **c.** 3
   Jon Hall

4. Grace Kelly/   **d.** 4
   Cary Grant

5. Joan Crawford/   **e.** 5
   Clark Gable

6. Margaret Sullavan/   **f.** 6
   James Stewart

7. Claudette Colbert/   **g.** 7
   Fred MacMurray

8. Shirley MacLaine/   **h.** 8
   Jack Lemmon

9. Loretta Young/   **i.** 9
   Tyrone Power

10. Ginger Rogers/   **j.** 10
    Fred Astaire

87. Match the co-stars of a famous film to the less-remembered film in which they had previously appeared together.

1. Merle Oberon and Laurence Olivier in *Wuthering Heights*

   a. *The Divorce of Lady X*

2. Carole Lombard and Fredric March in *Nothing Sacred*

   b. *A Yank at Oxford*

3. Marilyn Monroe and David Wayne in *How to Marry a Millionaire*

   c. *Me and My Gal*

4. Kathryn Grayson and Gene Kelly in *Anchors Aweigh*

   d. *Trouble for Two*

5. Joan Bennett and Spencer Tracy in *Father of the Bride*

   e. *Sylvia Scarlett*

6. Olivia de Havilland and Leslie Howard in *Gone With the Wind*

   f. *Thousands Cheer*

7. Vivien Leigh and Robert Taylor in *Waterloo Bridge*

   g. *The Secret Six*

8. Rosalind Russell and Robert Montgomery in *Night Must Fall*

   h. *We're Not Married*

9. Jean Harlow and Wallace Beery in *Dinner at Eight*

   i. *It's Love I'm After*

10. Katharine Hepburn and Cary Grant in *Bringing Up Baby*

   j. *The Eagle and the Hawk*

88. Who was not one of these titular threesomes?

1. *A Letter to Three Wives*
   a. Ann Sothern; b. Linda Darnell;
   c. Dorothy McGuire;
   d. Jeanne Crain

2. *Three Comrades*
   a. Walter Pidgeon; b. Franchot Tone;
   c. Robert Taylor; d. Robert Young

3. *These Three*
   a. Miriam Hopkins; b. Fredric March;
   c. Merle Oberon; d. Joel McCrea

4. *Three on a Match*
   a. Bette Davis; b. Ann Dvorak;
   c. Constance Bennett;
   d. Joan Blondell

5. *The Three Musketeers* (1948)
   a. Peter Lawford; b. Robert Coote;
   c. Gig Young; d. Van Heflin

6. *Three Little Girls in Blue*
   a. Vera-Ellen; b. Joan Caulfield;
   c. Vivian Blaine; d. June Haver

7. *Three Strangers*
   a. Peter Lorre; b. Sydney Greenstreet;
   c. Claude Rains;
   d. Geraldine Fitzgerald

8. *Three Guys Named Mike*
   a. Van Johnson; b. Howard Keel;
   c. Barry Sullivan; d. John Hodiak

9. *Three Godfathers*
   a. Victor McLaglen; b. John Wayne;
   c. Harry Carey, Jr.;
   d. Pedro Armendariz

10. *Tom, Dick and Harry*
    a. Alan Marshal; b. George Murphy,
    c. Burgess Meredith;
    d. Dennis Morgan

Gene Kelly and Judy Garland in *The Pirate*

EIGHT

"A Song to Remember"

89. Match the musical performer to the film in which he/she sang a song or two (before or after becoming famous).

1.	Nelson Eddy	**a.**	*Pete Kelly's Blues*
2.	Jeanette MacDonald	**b.**	*The Gay Divorcee*
3.	Howard Keel	**c.**	*Girl Crazy* (1943)
4.	Ella Fitzgerald	**d.**	*Follow the Boys*
5.	June Allyson	**e.**	*Deep in My Heart*
6.	Julie London	**f.**	*Panama Hattie*
7.	Louis Armstrong	**g.**	*Dancing Lady*
8.	Lena Horne	**h.**	*Sun Valley Serenade*
9.	Betty Grable	**i.**	*High Society*
10.	Dorothy Dandridge	**j.**	*The Girl Can't Help It*

90. Match the song standard to the film that introduced it.

1.	"I've Got My Love to Keep Me Warm"	**a.**	*Babes on Broadway*
2.	"Isn't It Romantic?"	**b.**	*Follow the Fleet*
3.	"Long Ago and Far Away"	**c.**	*Love Me Tonight*
4.	"How About You?"	**d.**	*Dames*
5.	"I've Got You Under My Skin"	**e.**	*A Damsel in Distress*
6.	"Let's Face the Music and Dance"	**f.**	*Gold Diggers of 1933*
7.	"They Can't Take That Away from Me"	**g.**	*On the Avenue*
8.	"A Foggy Day"	**h.**	*Cover Girl*
9.	"I Only Have Eyes for You"	**i.**	*Shall We Dance*
10.	"We're in the Money"	**j.**	*Born to Dance*

91. Match the song to the film for which it won an Oscar for Best Song.

1.	"You'll Never Know"	**a.**	*Hello, Frisco, Hello*
2.	"The Continental"	**b.**	*Lady Be Good*
3.	"Mona Lisa"	**c.**	*A Hole in the Head*
4.	"Buttons and Bows"	**d.**	*Going My Way*
5.	"The Last Time I Saw Paris"	**e.**	*Swing Time*
6.	"Thanks for the Memory"	**f.**	*The Gay Divorcee*
7.	"The Way You Look Tonight"	**g.**	*The Paleface*
8.	"Swinging on a Star"	**h.**	*Here Comes the Groom*
9.	"High Hopes"	**i.**	*Captain Carey, U.S.A.*
10.	"In the Cool, Cool, Cool of the Evening"	**j.**	*The Big Broadcast of 1938*

92. Match the singer to the film in which he/she provided the singing voice for the title tune or theme song.

1. Peggy Lee		**a.** *Friendly Persuasion*
2. Johnny Mathis		**b.** *High Noon*
3. Vic Damone		**c.** *Three Coins in the Fountain*
4. Pat Boone		**d.** *Johnny Guitar*
5. Nat "King" Cole		**e.** *Return to Peyton Place*
6. Tex Ritter		**f.** *The Best of Everything*
7. Rosemary Clooney		**g.** *Love with the Proper Stranger*
8. Frank Sinatra		**h.** *An Affair to Remember*
9. Jack Jones		**i.** *Thunderball*
10. Tom Jones		**j.** *Raintree County*

93. Match the screen adaptation of a Broadway musical to the song that was added to its score for the film version.

1. *Roberta*		**a.** "Anyone Here for Love?"
2. *Good News* (1947)		**b.** "Something Good"
3. *Gentlemen Prefer Blondes*		**c.** "Lovely to Look At"
4. *Guys and Dolls*		**d.** "Fated to Be Mated"
5. *On the Town*		**e.** "A Woman in Love"
6. *Damn Yankees*		**f.** "There's Something About an Empty Chair"
7. *The Sound of Music*		**g.** "Pass That Peace Pipe"
8. *Silk Stockings*		**h.** "You're Awful"
9. *South Pacific*		**i.** "I Have the Room Above Her"
10. *Show Boat* (1936)		**j.** "My Girl Back Home"

94. Match the Broadway composer to the film for which he wrote the music for original songs.

1. Jerome Kern	**a.** *Seven Brides for Seven Brothers*
2. Cole Porter	**b.** *Anchors Aweigh*
3. Gene de Paul	**c.** *Gigi*
4. Frank Loesser	**d.** *Centennial Summer*
5. Frederick Loewe	**e.** *A Damsel in Distress*
6. Jule Styne	**f.** *On the Avenue*
7. George Gershwin	**g.** *The Pirate*
8. Irving Berlin	**h.** *Hallelujah, I'm a Bum*
9. Richard Rodgers	**i.** *Hans Christian Andersen*
10. Kurt Weill	**j.** *Where Do We Go from Here?*

95. Match the song to the film in which it is sung by Marlene Dietrich.

1. "Falling in Love Again"	**a.** *Desire*
2. "You've Got That Look That Leaves Me Weak"	**b.** *Seven Sinners*
3. "What Am I Bid for My Apples?"	**c.** *A Foreign Affair*
4. "I Can't Give You Anything But Love"	**d.** *Blonde Venus*
5. "Hot Voodoo"	**e.** *Stage Fright*
6. "The Laziest Gal in Town"	**f.** *Destry Rides Again*
7. "Awake in a Dream"	**g.** *The Flame of New Orleans*
8. "Sweet Is the Blush of May"	**h.** *The Blue Angel*
9. "Get Away Young Man"	**i.** *Rancho Notorious*
10. "Black Market"	**j.** *Morocco*

96. Match the song to the film in which it is sung by Frank Sinatra.

1.	"All My Tomorrows"	**a.**	*Anchors Aweigh*
2.	"The Lady Is a Tramp"	**b.**	*A Hole in the Head*
3.	"All the Way"	**c.**	*Young at Heart*
4.	"I Fall in Love Too Easily"	**d.**	*Guys and Dolls*
5.	"Time After Time"	**e.**	*Pal Joey*
6.	"Sue Me"	**f.**	*Higher and Higher*
7.	"You're Sensational"	**g.**	*It Happened in Brooklyn*
8.	"Just One of Those Things"	**h.**	*Robin and the Seven Hoods*
9.	"My Kind of Town"	**i.**	*The Joker Is Wild*
10.	"I Couldn't Sleep a Wink Last Night"	**j.**	*High Society*

97. Match the song to the usually nonsinging performers who sing it (in an informal setting) in a movie.

1.	"Night and Day"	**a.**	Audrey Hepburn in *Sabrina*
2.	"Over the Rainbow"	**b.**	Jack Lemmon and Judy Holliday in *It Should Happen to You*
3.	"Swanee River"	**c.**	Katharine Hepburn in *Desk Set*
4.	"After You've Gone"	**d.**	James Stewart and Donna Reed in *It's a Wonderful Life*
5.	"I Can't Give You Anything But Love"	**e.**	James Stewart in *The Philadelphia Story*
6.	"Yes! We Have No Bananas"	**f.**	Bette Davis in *Dead Ringer*
7.	"Buffalo Gals"	**g.**	Clark Gable in *It Happened One Night*
8.	"Who's Afraid of the Big Bad Wolf?"	**h.**	Shirley MacLaine in *Some Came Running*
9.	"Shuffle Off to Buffalo"	**i.**	Jean Arthur in *Mr. Deeds Goes to Town*
10.	"Let's Fall in Love"	**j.**	Cary Grant and Katharine Hepburn in *Bringing Up Baby*

James Cagney and Olivia de Havilland in *The Strawberry Blonde*

"Boy Meets Girl"

98. Match the actress to the film in which she appeared with James Cagney.

1.	Jean Harlow	**a.**	*The Roaring Twenties*
2.	Rita Hayworth	**b.**	*These Wilder Years*
3.	Sylvia Sidney	**c.**	*The Public Enemy*
4.	Gladys George	**d.**	*White Heat*
5.	Ann Sheridan	**e.**	*Man of a Thousand Faces*
6.	Virginia Mayo	**f.**	*The Strawberry Blonde*
7.	Dorothy Malone	**g.**	*Jimmy the Gent*
8.	Bette Davis	**h.**	*Angels with Dirty Faces*
9.	Gloria Stuart	**i.**	*Blood on the Sun*
10.	Barbara Stanwyck	**j.**	*Here Comes the Navy*

99. Match the actor to the film in which he appeared with Myrna Loy.

1.	Montgomery Clift	**a.**	*Too Hot to Handle*
2.	Clark Gable	**b.**	*The Rains Came*
3.	John Barrymore	**c.**	*Broadway Bill*
4.	Warner Baxter	**d.**	*Love Crazy*
5.	Paul Newman	**e.**	*Lonelyhearts*
6.	Ronald Colman	**f.**	*From the Terrace*
7.	Tyrone Power	**g.**	*Love Me Tonight*
8.	William Powell	**h.**	*Topaze*
9.	Maurice Chevalier	**i.**	*Arrowsmith*
10.	Leslie Howard	**j.**	*The Animal Kingdom*

100. Match the actress to the film in which she appeared with Henry Fonda.

1. Ginger Rogers	**a.**	*The Story of Alexander Graham Bell*
2. Barbara Stanwyck	**b.**	*That Certain Woman*
3. Margaret Sullavan	**c.**	*The Farmer Takes a Wife*
4. Linda Darnell	**d.**	*Tales of Manhattan*
5. Sylvia Sidney	**e.**	*Chad Hanna*
6. Janet Gaynor	**f.**	*The Male Animal*
7. Bette Davis	**g.**	*The Mad Miss Manton*
8. Loretta Young	**h.**	*The Big Street*
9. Olivia de Havilland	**i.**	*The Moon's Our Home*
10. Lucille Ball	**j.**	*You Only Live Once*

101. Match the actor to the film in which he appeared with Ginger Rogers.

1. James Stewart	**a.**	*Having Wonderful Time*
2. Joel McCrea	**b.**	*It Had to Be You*
3. Ray Milland	**c.**	*Primrose Path*
4. Cary Grant	**d.**	*Weekend at the Waldorf*
5. Walter Pidgeon	**e.**	*Once Upon A Honeymoon*
6. Ronald Colman	**f.**	*Tight Spot*
7. Douglas Fairbanks, Jr.	**g.**	*Vivacious Lady*
8. Clifton Webb	**h.**	*Lucky Partners*
9. Cornel Wilde	**i.**	*The Major and the Minor*
10. Edward G. Robinson	**j.**	*Dreamboat*

102. Match the actress to the film in which she appeared with Bob Hope.

1. Katharine Hepburn	**a.** *My Favorite Spy*
2. Lucille Ball	**b.** *My Favorite Blonde*
3. Madeleine Carroll	**c.** *My Favorite Brunette*
4. Eva Marie Saint	**d.** *That Certain Feeling*
5. Arlene Dahl	**e.** *The Iron Petticoat*
6. Dorothy Lamour	**f.** *Fancy Pants*
7. Rhonda Fleming	**g.** *Nothing But the Truth*
8. Hedy Lamarr	**h.** *Let's Face It*
9. Paulette Goddard	**i.** *The Great Lover*
10. Betty Hutton	**j.** *Here Come the Girls*

103. Match the actor to the film in which he appeared with Ingrid Bergman.

1. Jose Ferrer	**a.** *Anastasia*
2. Gary Cooper	**b.** *Joan of Arc*
3. Cary Grant	**c.** *Rage in Heaven*
4. Robert Montgomery	**d.** *The Inn of the Sixth Happiness*
5. Anthony Perkins	**e.** *Arch of Triumph*
6. Yul Brynner	**f.** *The Yellow Rolls-Royce*
7. Charles Boyer	**g.** *Indiscreet*
8. Joseph Cotten	**h.** *Goodbye Again*
9. Omar Sharif	**i.** *Saratoga Trunk*
10. Curt Jurgens	**j.** *Under Capricorn*

104. Match the actress to the film in which she appeared with William Holden.

1.	Grace Kelly	**a.**	*Escape from Fort Bravo*
2.	Deborah Kerr	**b.**	*Forever Female*
3.	Jeanne Crain	**c.**	*The Counterfeit Traitor*
4.	Veronica Lake	**d.**	*The Bridges at Toko-Ri*
5.	Lilli Palmer	**e.**	*The Proud and the Profane*
6.	Loretta Young	**f.**	*The Key*
7.	Lucille Ball	**g.**	*Apartment for Peggy*
8.	Sophia Loren	**h.**	*Rachel and the Stranger*
9.	Ginger Rogers	**i.**	*I Wanted Wings*
10.	Eleanor Parker	**j.**	*Miss Grant Takes Richmond*

105. Match the actor to the film in which he appeared with Betty Grable.

1.	Victor Mature	**a.**	*How to Marry a Millionaire*
2.	Tyrone Power	**b.**	*Three for the Show*
3.	Jack Lemmon	**c.**	*How to Be Very, Very Popular*
4.	Rory Calhoun	**d.**	*Mother Wore Tights*
5.	Douglas Fairbanks, Jr.	**e.**	*A Yank in the R.A.F.*
6.	Dan Dailey	**f.**	*Billy Rose's Diamond Horseshoe*
7.	Robert Young	**g.**	*The Dolly Sisters*
8.	Robert Cummings	**h.**	*Wabash Avenue*
9.	John Payne	**i.**	*That Lady in Ermine*
10.	Dick Haymes	**j.**	*Sweet Rosie O'Grady*

106. Match the actress to the film in which she appeared with Gregory Peck.

1.	Greer Garson	**a.**	*The Great Sinner*
2.	Joan Bennett	**b.**	*Yellow Sky*
3.	Sophia Loren	**c.**	*The Macomber Affair*
4.	Deborah Kerr	**d.**	*Captain Horatio Hornblower*
5.	Jean Simmons	**e.**	*The Valley of Decision*
6.	Ava Gardner	**f.**	*The Big Country*
7.	Virginia Mayo	**g.**	*Designing Woman*
8.	Jennifer Jones	**h.**	*Beloved Infidel*
9.	Anne Baxter	**i.**	*Arabesque*
10.	Lauren Bacall	**j.**	*The Man in the Gray Flannel Suit*

107. Match the actor to the film in which he appeared with Doris Day.

1. James Cagney	**a.** *Please Don't Eat the Daisies*
2. Louis Jourdan	**b.** *The Winning Team*
3. David Niven	**c.** *Teacher's Pet*
4. Rex Harrison	**d.** *The West Point Story*
5. Clark Gable	**e.** *I'll See You in My Dreams*
6. Richard Widmark	**f.** *The Tunnel of Love*
7. Jack Lemmon	**g.** *Julie*
8. Danny Thomas	**h.** *Lover Come Back*
9. Ronald Reagan	**i.** *It Happened to Jane*
10. Rock Hudson	**j.** *Midnight Lace*

Bette Davis in *The Star*

TEN

"Golden Boy"

108. Match the film to the Academy Award it received.

1.	*Citizen Kane*	**a.**	1937 Best Actress
2.	*The Great Ziegfeld*	**b.**	1936 Best Director
3.	*The Good Earth*	**c.**	1937 Best Actor
4.	*Rebecca*	**d.**	1940 Best Director
5.	*Captains Courageous*	**e.**	1936 Best Picture
6.	*The Grapes of Wrath*	**f.**	1941 Best Picture
7.	*The Awful Truth*	**g.**	1937 Best Picture
8.	*The Life of Emile Zola*	**h.**	1941 Best Original Screenplay
9.	*How Green Was My Valley*	**i.**	1937 Best Director
10.	*Mr. Deeds Goes to Town*	**j.**	1940 Best Picture

109. The following stars won many Oscar nominations. For each, pick the one performance that was not nominated.

1. Greer Garson
   - **a.** *Goodbye, Mr. Chips;*
   - **b.** *Pride and Prejudice;*
   - **c.** *Blossoms in the Dust;*
   - **d.** *Madame Curie*

2. Paul Newman
   - **a.** *Hud;* **b.** *The Hustler;*
   - **c.** *Somebody Up There Likes Me;*
   - **d.** *Cool Hand Luke*

3. Richard Burton
   - **a.** *The Robe;*
   - **b.** *The Night of the Iguana;*
   - **c.** *The Spy Who Came in from the Cold;*
   - **d.** *My Cousin Rachel*

4. Greta Garbo
   - **a.** *Anna Christie;* **b.** *Romance;*
   - **c.** *Grand Hotel;* **d.** *Ninotchka*

5. Bette Davis
   - **a.** *Of Human Bondage;* **b.** *The Star;*
   - **c.** *The Letter;* **d.** *Mr. Skeffington*

6. Paul Muni
   - **a.** *Scarface;* **b.** *The Last Angry Man;*
   - **c.** *The Life of Emile Zola;*
   - **d.** *The Story of Louis Pasteur*

7. Shirley MacLaine
   - **a.** *Some Came Running;*
   - **b.** *Irma La Douce;* **c.** *The Apartment;*
   - **d.** *The Children's Hour*

8. Elizabeth Taylor
   - **a.** *Cat on a Hot Tin Roof;*
   - **b.** *Raintree County;*
   - **c.** *Suddenly, Last Summer;* **d.** *Giant*

9. Katharine Hepburn
   - **a.** *Woman of the Year;* **b.** *Little Women;*
   - **c.** *The Rainmaker;*
   - **d.** *Suddenly, Last Summer*

10. Mickey Rooney
    - **a.** *National Velvet;* **b.** *Babes in Arms;*
    - **c.** *The Human Comedy;*
    - **d.** *The Bold and the Brave*

110. Pick the film for which each man won a Best Director Oscar.

1. Vincente Minnelli   **a.** *Meet Me in St. Louis;*
   b. *Lust for Life;*
   c. *An American in Paris;* **d.** *Gigi*

2. George Cukor   **a.** *Camille;* **b.** *The Women;*
   c. *Gaslight;* **d.** *My Fair Lady*

3. John Ford   **a.** *Stagecoach;*
   b. *My Darling Clementine;*
   c. *The Quiet Man;* **d.** *The Searchers*

4. Victor Fleming   **a.** *Gone With the Wind;*
   b. *The Wizard of Oz;*
   c. *Captains Courageous;* **d.** *Joan of Arc*

5. Michael Curtiz   **a.** *Angels with Dirty Faces;*
   b. *Casablanca;*
   c. *Yankee Doodle Dandy;*
   d. *Mildred Pierce*

6. George Stevens   **a.** *Gunga Din;* **b.** *Shane;*
   c. *The More the Merrier;* **d.** *Giant*

7. John Huston   **a.** *The Treasure of the Sierra Madre;*
   b. *Moby Dick;* **c.** *The Maltese Falcon;*
   d. *The African Queen*

8. Billy Wilder   **a.** *Double Indemnity;*
   b. *The Lost Weekend;*
   c. *Sunset Boulevard;*
   d. *Some Like It Hot*

9. Elia Kazan   **a.** *A Tree Grows in Brooklyn;*
   b. *East of Eden;* **c.** *On the Waterfront;*
   d. *A Streetcar Named Desire*

10. Carol Reed   **a.** *Oliver!;* **b.** *Odd Man Out;*
   c. *The Fallen Idol;* **d.** *The Third Man*

111. Pick the film for which each performer won an Oscar for a supporting role.

1. Gloria Grahame
   a. *It's a Wonderful Life;*
   b. *In a Lonely Place;*
   c. *The Big Heat;*
   d. *The Bad and the Beautiful*

2. Van Heflin
   a. *Johnny Eager;* b. *Battle Cry;*
   c. *Shane;* d. *Airport*

3. Teresa Wright
   a. *The Pride of the Yankees;*
   b. *Mrs. Miniver;* c. *The Little Foxes;*
   d. *The Best Years of Our Lives*

4. Karl Malden
   a. *On the Waterfront;*
   b. *Fear Strikes Out;*
   c. *A Streetcar Named Desire;*
   d. *One-Eyed Jacks*

5. Anne Baxter
   a. *The Magnificent Ambersons;*
   b. *The Razor's Edge;*
   c. *All About Eve;*
   d. *The Ten Commandments*

6. Edmond O'Brien
   a. *The Barefoot Contessa;*
   b. *Julius Caesar;* c. *The Killers;*
   d. *Seven Days in May*

7. Mary Astor
   a. *Dodsworth;* b. *The Maltese Falcon;*
   c. *The Great Lie;*
   d. *Meet Me in St. Louis*

8. Anne Revere
   a. *The Song of Bernadette;*
   b. *Body and Soul;*
   c. *Gentleman's Agreement;*
   d. *National Velvet*

9. Walter Huston
   a. *And Then There Were None;*
   b. *Duel in the Sun;*
   c. *The Treasure of the Sierra Madre;*
   d. *Of Human Hearts*

10. Ethel Barrymore
    a. *None But the Lonely Heart;*
    b. *Pinky;* c. *The Farmer's Daughter;*
    d. *The Spiral Staircase*

112. Pick the film for which each star received his/her only Oscar nomination for acting.

1. Lana Turner
    a. *Imitation of Life;* **b.** *Peyton Place;*
    c. *The Postman Always Rings Twice;*
    d. *The Bad and the Beautiful*

2. Ava Gardner
    a. *Mogambo;* **b.** *Show Boat;*
    c. *On the Beach;*
    d. *The Night of the Iguana*

3. Gene Kelly
    a. *Anchors Aweigh;* **b.** *On the Town;*
    c. *An American in Paris;*
    d. *Singin' in the Rain*

4. Anthony Perkins
    a. *Psycho;* **b.** *Desire Under the Elms;*
    c. *Fear Strikes Out;*
    d. *Friendly Persuasion*

5. Carole Lombard
    a. *Twentieth Century;*
    b. *Nothing Sacred;* **c.** *My Man Godfrey;*
    d. *To Be or Not to Be*

6. Tony Curtis
    a. *The Defiant Ones;*
    b. *Sweet Smell of Success;*
    c. *Some Like It Hot;*
    d. *The Boston Strangler*

7. Jean Arthur
    a. *Shane;* **b.** *The More the Merrier;*
    c. *Mr. Deeds Goes to Town;*
    d. *The Talk of the Town*

8. Robert Mitchum
    a. *Ryan's Daughter;*
    b. *The Sundowners;*
    c. *The Story of G.I. Joe;*
    d. *Heaven Knows, Mr. Allison*

9. Orson Welles
    a. *Jane Eyre;* **b.** *The Stranger;*
    c. *Citizen Kane;* **d.** *Touch of Evil*

10. Dorothy McGuire
    a. *Friendly Persuasion;*
    b. *A Tree Grows in Brooklyn;*
    c. *The Spiral Staircase;*
    d. *Gentleman's Agreement*

113. Match the actor to the year in which he received his only Oscar nomination for acting. Name the film as well. Also, name the only winner in the group (special Oscars don't count).

1.	Fred Astaire	**a.**	1937
2.	Robert Preston	**b.**	1940
3.	Rock Hudson	**c.**	1945
4.	Raymond Massey	**d.**	1950
5.	Ralph Bellamy	**e.**	1956
6.	Jeff Chandler	**f.**	1960
7.	Cornel Wilde	**g.**	1966
8.	John Mills	**h.**	1970
9.	Trevor Howard	**i.**	1974
10.	Steve McQueen	**j.**	1982

114. Match the actress to the year in which she received her only Oscar nomination for acting. Name the film as well. Also, name the only winner in the group (special Oscars don't count).

1.	Sylvia Sidney	a.	1930/31
2.	Lee Remick	b.	1935
3.	Lillian Gish	c.	1940
4.	Joan Blondell	d.	1946
5.	Peggy Ashcroft	e.	1951
6.	Merle Oberon	f.	1956
7.	Ann Sothern	g.	1962
8.	Martha Scott	h.	1973
9.	Marlene Dietrich	i.	1984
10.	Carroll Baker	j.	1987

115. Match the usually supporting player to the film for which he/she received a Best Actor/Best Actress Oscar nomination. Then name the only winner in the group.

1.	Monty Woolley	a.	*Wilson*
2.	Gladys George	b.	*The Front Page* (1931)
3.	Adolphe Menjou	c.	*Adventures of Robinson Crusoe*
4.	May Robson	d.	*The Pied Piper*
5.	Louis Calhern	e.	*Watch on the Rhine*
6.	Edith Evans	f.	*The Affairs of Cellini*
7.	Alexander Knox	g.	*The Whisperers*
8.	Paul Lukas	h.	*Lady for a Day*
9.	Dan O'Herlihy	i.	*Valiant Is the Word for Carrie*
10.	Frank Morgan	j.	*The Magnificent Yankee*

116. Match the actress to the role that won her an Oscar. Then name the film.

1.	Ingrid Bergman	a.	Gloria Wandrous
2.	Anne Bancroft	b.	Lola Delaney
3.	Grace Kelly	c.	Paula Alquist
4.	Katharine Hepburn	d.	Ellie Andrews
5.	Shirley Booth	e.	Christina Drayton
6.	Eva Marie Saint	f.	Catherine Sloper
7.	Elizabeth Taylor	g.	Annie Sullivan
8.	Claudette Colbert	h.	Marylee Hadley
9.	Olivia de Havilland	i.	Edie Doyle
10.	Dorothy Malone	j.	Georgie Elgin

117. Match the Best Actor Academy Award performance to the actress who appeared with the actor in that film.

1. Gary Cooper in *Sergeant York*	**a.** Jane Wyman
2. Paul Scofield in *A Man for All Seasons*	**b.** Mala Powers
3. Charlton Heston in *Ben-Hur*	**c.** Lilia Skala
4. Ernest Borgnine in *Marty*	**d.** Wendy Hiller
5. Sidney Poitier in *Lilies of the Field*	**e.** Betsy Blair
6. Ray Milland in *The Lost Weekend*	**f.** Haya Harareet
7. Jose Ferrer in *Cyrano de Bergerac*	**g.** Joanne Dru
8. Laurence Olivier in *Hamlet*	**h.** Joan Bennett
9. George Arliss in *Disraeli*	**i.** Jean Simmons
10. Broderick Crawford in *All the King's Men*	**j.** Joan Leslie

118. Match the Best Actress Academy Award performance to the actor who appeared with the actress in that film.

1. Jane Wyman in *Johnny Belinda*

2. Joanne Woodward in *The Three Faces of Eve*

3. Judy Holliday in *Born Yesterday*

4. Janet Gaynor in *Seventh Heaven*

5. Ginger Rogers in *Kitty Foyle*

6. Katharine Hepburn in *Morning Glory*

7. Bette Davis in *Dangerous*

8. Loretta Young in *The Farmer's Daughter*

9. Joan Crawford in *Mildred Pierce*

10. Norma Shearer in *The Divorcee*

a. David Wayne

b. Franchot Tone

c. Charles Farrell

d. Jack Carson

e. Douglas Fairbanks, Jr.

f. William Holden

g. Chester Morris

h. Lew Ayres

i. Dennis Morgan

j. Joseph Cotten

119. Match the star to the Oscar-related fact which describes him/her.

1. Joan Fontaine	**a.** Lost an Oscar to a sibling.
2. Walter Brennan	**b.** Got a Best Actress nomination for playing Jane Hudson.
3. Peter O'Toole	**c.** First performer to win an Oscar for a color film.
4. Audrey Hepburn	**d.** Nominated for a film directed by a spouse.
5. Olivia de Havilland	**e.** Only performer to win an Oscar for a Hitchcock film.
6. Raymond Massey	**f.** Nominated in 1954 for a role played on Broadway by Margaret Sullavan.
7. Arthur Kennedy	**g.** He and his son won nominations for playing real people.
8. Jean Simmons	**h.** Nominated for a musical remake of a film that won another performer an Oscar.
9. Richard Burton	**i.** Nominated for four films directed by the same man.
10. Katharine Hepburn	**j.** Nominated for a role that had previously won an Oscar for Charles Laughton.

Robert Taylor and Vivien Leigh in *Waterloo Bridge*

ELEVEN

"Once Is Not Enough"

120. Match the Irene Dunne film to the actress who would reprise her role in a remake of that film. I hope Irene was flattered by the number of her films that were deemed remake-worthy (I didn't even include *Show Boat* and *Anna and the King of Siam*).

1. *Roberta*
2. *Love Affair*
3. *A Guy Named Joe*
4. *The Awful Truth*
5. *My Favorite Wife*
6. *Cimarron*
7. *Back Street*
8. *When Tomorrow Comes*
9. *The Age of Innocence*
10. *Magnificent Obsession*

a. Jane Wyman (with Ray Milland)
b. Jane Wyman (with Rock Hudson)
c. Doris Day
d. Kathryn Grayson
e. Deborah Kerr
f. Michelle Pfeiffer
g. June Allyson
h. Maria Schell
i. Margaret Sullavan
j. Holly Hunter

121. Match the MGM performance on the left to its MGM remake on the right.

1. Jean Harlow in
   Red Dust

2. Norma Shearer in
   The Women

3. Greta Garbo in
   Grand Hotel

4. Margaret Sullavan
   in *The Shop Around
   the Corner*

5. Jean Harlow in
   Libeled Lady

6. Greta Garbo in
   Ninotchka

7. Katharine Hepburn
   in *The Philadelphia
   Story*

8. Vivien Leigh in
   Waterloo Bridge

9. Norma Shearer in
   A Free Soul

10. Joan Crawford in
    *The Last of Mrs.
    Cheyney*

a. Judy Garland in *In the Good Old
Summertime*

b. Leslie Caron in *Gaby*

c. Ava Gardner in *Mogambo*

d. Grace Kelly in *High Society*

e. Lucille Ball in *Easy to Wed*

f. June Allyson in *The Opposite Sex*

g. Greer Garson in *The Law and
the Lady*

h. Elizabeth Taylor in *The Girl Who
Had Everything*

i. Ginger Rogers in *Weekend at the
Waldorf*

j. Cyd Charisse in *Silk Stockings*

122. Match the performance on the left to its remake on the right.

1. Ginger Rogers in *The Major and the Minor*

   a. Sydney Greenstreet in *The Maltese Falcon*

2. Maureen O'Hara in *Sentimental Journey*

   b. Jerry Lewis in *Living It Up*

3. Pat O'Brien in *The Front Page*

   c. Sandra Dee in *I'd Rather Be Rich*

4. Alison Skipworth in *Satan Met a Lady*

   d. Susan Hayward in *Stolen Hours*

5. Kay Francis in *One Way Passage*

   e. Merle Oberon in *'Til We Meet Again*

6. Robert Cummings in *It Started with Eve*

   f. Betty Grable in *Wabash Avenue*

7. Barbara Stanwyck in *The Lady Eve*

   g. Jerry Lewis in *You're Never Too Young*

8. Carole Lombard in *Nothing Sacred*

   h. Lauren Bacall in *The Gift of Love*

9. Bette Davis in *Dark Victory*

   i. Rosalind Russell in *His Girl Friday*

10. Betty Grable in *Coney Island*

   j. Mitzi Gaynor in *The Birds and the Bees*

123. Match the film to the actress who starred in a remake of that film in the year listed by her name. Some of the remakes kept the original title and some did not.

1. *The Broadway Melody* (1929) **a.** Ann Sheridan (1940)

2. *Of Human Bondage* (1934) **b.** Simone Simon (1937)

3. *Red Dust* (1932) **c.** Shelley Winters (1951)

4. *Libeled Lady* (1936) **d.** Ann Sothern (1940)

5. *A Bill of Divorcement* (1932) **e.** Esther Williams (1946)

6. *The Maltese Falcon* (1931) **f.** Eleanor Parker (1946)

7. *Seventh Heaven* (1927) **g.** Bette Davis (1936)

8. *20,000 Years in Sing Sing* (1933) **h.** Gladys George (1937)

9. *Madame X* (1929) **i.** Joan Blondell (1940)

10. *An American Tragedy* (1931) **j.** Maureen O'Hara (1940)

124. Each actor on the left made a well-known film in the year listed by his name. Match each actor to the one on the right who played the same role in a remake of that film (made in the year listed by his name). How about naming the films too?

1. Charles Laughton (1934)
2. Fredric March (1937)
3. Leslie Howard (1938)
4. Robert Donat (1939)
5. Cary Grant (1940)
6. Melvyn Douglas (1939)
7. Clark Gable (1932)
8. Clark Gable (1935)
9. James Stewart (1940)
10. Wallace Beery (1931)

a. James Mason (1954)
b. Peter O'Toole (1969)
c. Fred Astaire (1957)
d. John Gielgud (1957)
e. Clark Gable (1953)
f. Marlon Brando (1962)
g. Bing Crosby (1956)
h. Rex Harrison (1964)
i. Van Johnson (1949)
j. Jon Voight (1979)

125. Match the Oscar-winning performance on the left to the actor who played the same role in a later film (not necessarily a remake).

1. Charles Coburn in *The More the Merrier*   **a.** Bing Crosby

2. Walter Brennan in *The Westerner*   **b.** Jack Lemmon

3. Thomas Mitchell in *Stagecoach*   **c.** Cesar Romero

4. Warner Baxter in *In Old Arizona*   **d.** William Powell

5. James Stewart in *The Philadelphia Story*   **e.** Cary Grant

6. George Arliss in *Disraeli*   **f.** Robert Shaw

7. Lionel Barrymore in *A Free Soul*   **g.** Alec Guinness

8. Charles Laughton in *The Private Life of Henry VIII*   **h.** Paul Newman

9. Clark Gable in *It Happened One Night*   **i.** Spencer Tracy

10. Fredric March in *Dr. Jekyll and Mr. Hyde*   **j.** Frank Sinatra

126. Match the popular film vehicle to the actor who starred in a 1920s silent version.

1.	*The Great Gatsby*	**a.**	Rudolph Valentino
2.	*Beau Geste*	**b.**	Warner Baxter
3.	*The Ten Commandments*	**c.**	Lewis Stone
4.	*Dr. Jekyll and Mr. Hyde*	**d.**	Douglas Fairbanks
5.	*The Prisoner of Zenda*	**e.**	Ronald Colman
6.	*The Merry Widow*	**f.**	Lon Chaney
7.	*Blood and Sand*	**g.**	John Barrymore
8.	*The Mark of Zorro*	**h.**	H. B. Warner
9.	*The Hunchback of Notre Dame*	**i.**	John Gilbert
10.	*The King of Kings*	**j.**	Richard Dix

127. Match the comedy to the performer who starred in its musical (or semi-musical) remake. Can you name the remake as well?

1.	*Ah, Wilderness!*	**a.**	Debbie Reynolds
2.	*Ball of Fire*	**b.**	Gordon MacRae
3.	*It Happened One Night*	**c.**	Danny Kaye
4.	*Bachelor Mother*	**d.**	Dorothy Lamour
5.	*Tom, Dick and Harry*	**e.**	Deanna Durbin
6.	*Midnight*	**f.**	Mickey Rooney
7.	*Too Many Husbands*	**g.**	Betty Grable
8.	*The Good Fairy*	**h.**	Nelson Eddy
9.	*Brother Rat*	**i.**	June Allyson
10.	*The Guardsman*	**j.**	Jane Powell

128. Films are often remade with the same title. Match each title on the left to the years in which two films with that title were released.

1.	*My Man Godfrey*	a.	1942/1983
2.	*Imitation of Life*	b.	1935/1954
3.	*Magnificent Obsession*	c.	1931/1960
4.	*To Be or Not to Be*	d.	1930/1938
5.	*Cimarron*	e.	1942/1955
6.	*Stagecoach*	f.	1936/1957
7.	*My Sister Eileen*	g.	1932/1957
8.	*Holiday*	h.	1934/1959
9.	*Lost Horizon*	i.	1937/1973
10.	*A Farewell to Arms*	j.	1939/1966

129. Match the film to the description of an earlier, unrelated film with the exact same title.

1.	*Carrie* (1976)	a.	1939 Bob Hope comedy
2.	*No Way Out* (1987)	b.	1948 Loretta Young drama
3.	*The Accused* (1988)	c.	1950 Robert Preston western
4.	*The Turning Point* (1977)	d.	1952 Laurence Olivier drama
5.	*Some Like It Hot* (1959)	e.	1931 Marx Brothers comedy
6.	*The Farmer's Daughter* (1947)	f.	1950 Richard Widmark drama
7.	*The Fugitive* (1993)	g.	1941 Loretta Young comedy
8.	*Monkey Business* (1952)	h.	1940 Martha Raye comedy
9.	*A Night to Remember* (1958)	i.	1952 William Holden drama
10.	*The Sundowners* (1960)	j.	1947 Henry Fonda drama

130. Match the actor to the role he played in at least two films.

1.	Walter Pidgeon	**a.**	James Hardy
2.	Spencer Tracy	**b.**	Bill Seacroft
3.	Lew Ayres	**c.**	Nick Charles
4.	Lewis Stone	**d.**	Stanley Banks
5.	Mickey Rooney	**e.**	Marion Hargrove
6.	Henry Fonda	**f.**	Clem Miniver
7.	William Holden	**g.**	Frank James
8.	William Powell	**h.**	Whitey Marsh
9.	Robert Walker	**i.**	William Sherman
10.	Gordon MacRae	**j.**	James Kildare

131. It is rare for a director to remake one of his own hits. Match each filmmaker to the two versions of the same story that he directed.

1.	Alfred Hitchcock	**a.**	*The Man Who Knew Too Much* (1934 and 1956)
2.	Leo McCarey	**b.**	*The Strawberry Blonde* (1941) *One Sunday Afternoon* (1948)
3.	Frank Capra	**c.**	*Destry Rides Again* (1939) *Destry* (1954)
4.	William Wyler	**d.**	*Midnight* (1939) *Masquerade in Mexico* (1945)
5.	Raoul Walsh	**e.**	*Lady for a Day* (1933) *Pocketful of Miracles* (1961)
6.	Mitchell Leisen	**f.**	*The Barretts of Wimpole Street* (1934 and 1957)
7.	Howard Hawks	**g.**	*Love Affair* (1939) *An Affair to Remember* (1957)
8.	Sidney Franklin	**h.**	*Ball of Fire* (1941) *A Song Is Born* (1948)
9.	George Marshall	**i.**	*The Ten Commandments* (1923 and 1956)
10.	Cecil B. DeMille	**j.**	*These Three* (1936) *The Children's Hour* (1961)

Kirk Douglas in *The Bad and the Beautiful*

TWELVE

"I Am a Camera"

132. Match the director to one of the jobs he had before he sat in the director's chair.

1.	Robert Wise	**a.**	Producer of *High Noon*
2.	Joseph L. Mankiewicz	**b.**	Cast member of *City for Conquest*
3.	Elia Kazan	**c.**	Co-writer of *Cobra Woman*
4.	David Lean	**d.**	Costume designer of *The Thief of Bagdad* (1924)
5.	Stanley Kramer	**e.**	Producer of *The Philadelphia Story*
6.	Richard Brooks	**f.**	Film editor of *Cat People* (1942)
7.	Sam Peckinpah	**g.**	Film editor of *Pygmalion*
8.	Mark Robson	**h.**	Co-writer of *Jezebel*
9.	Mitchell Leisen	**i.**	Film editor of *Citizen Kane*
10.	John Huston	**j.**	Cast member of *Invasion of the Body Snatchers* (1956)

133. Match the film and one of its directors to the man who co-directed it. Some of these pairs worked as teams and some came about when one man finished a film started by another.

    1. *Singin' in the Rain*   **a.** Noël Coward
       —Gene Kelly

    2. *Mister Roberts*   **b.** Howard Hawks
       —Mervyn LeRoy

    3. *The Red Shoes*—   **c.** John Ford
       Emeric Pressburger

    4. *In Which We Serve*   **d.** Anthony Asquith
       —David Lean

    5. *The Pajama Game*   **e.** Stanley Donen
       —Stanley Donen

    6. *The Court Jester*   **f.** Michael Curtiz
       —Melvin Frank

    7. *Come and Get It*   **g.** Jerome Robbins
       —William Wyler

    8. *Pygmalion*—   **h.** George Abbott
       Leslie Howard

    9. *West Side Story*   **i.** Michael Powell
       —Robert Wise

  10. *The Adventures*   **j.** Norman Panama
       of Robin Hood—
       William Keighley

134. Match the very famous film to the not very famous man who directed it.

1.	*Sweet Smell of Success*	**a.**	Robert Z. Leonard
2.	*Gilda*	**b.**	Frank Tuttle
3.	*To Kill a Mockingbird*	**c.**	Michael Gordon
4.	*This Gun for Hire*	**d.**	Sam Wood
5.	*Top Hat*	**e.**	Alexander Mackendrick
6.	*Pride and Prejudice*	**f.**	Delbert Mann
7.	*Marty*	**g.**	Robert Mulligan
8.	*For Whom the Bell Tolls*	**h.**	Irving Rapper
9.	*Now, Voyager*	**i.**	Mark Sandrich
10.	*Pillow Talk*	**j.**	Charles Vidor

135. Match the horror or sci-fi classic to the man who directed it.

1. *I Walked With a Zombie*   **a.** Roman Polanski

2. *Invasion of the Body Snatchers* (1956)   **b.** Mark Robson

3. *The Day the Earth Stood Still*   **c.** Andre de Toth

4. *Bride of Frankenstein*   **d.** Tod Browning

5. *Repulsion*   **e.** Robert Wise

6. *House of Wax*   **f.** Don Siegel

7. *Seconds*   **g.** James Whale

8. *Dr. Jekyll and Mr. Hyde* (1932)   **h.** John Frankenheimer

9. *Dracula* (1931)   **i.** Jacques Tourneur

10. *Isle of the Dead*   **j.** Rouben Mamoulian

136. Match the director to the star he directed in at least four films.

1. Billy Wilder   **a.** Barbara Stanwyck

2. Michael Curtiz   **b.** Miriam Hopkins

3. Cecil B. DeMille   **c.** James Stewart

4. Busby Berkeley   **d.** William Holden

5. Joseph L. Mankiewicz   **e.** Jeanette MacDonald

6. Fritz Lang   **f.** Judy Garland

7. Alfred Hitchcock   **g.** Doris Day

8. Frank Capra   **h.** Rex Harrison

9. William Wyler   **i.** Joan Bennett

10. Ernst Lubitsch   **j.** Gary Cooper

137. George Cukor hated being called "a woman's director." So let's avoid Kate, Garbo and *The Women* for the moment. Match the actor to the Cukor film in which he appeared.

1. Anthony Quinn		**a.**	*Gaslight*
2. Spencer Tracy		**b.**	*Susan and God*
3. Ray Milland		**c.**	*Holiday*
4. Fredric March		**d.**	*Heller in Pink Tights*
5. Melvyn Douglas		**e.**	*A Woman's Face*
6. Joseph Cotten		**f.**	*Little Women*
7. Stewart Granger		**g.**	*A Bill of Divorcement*
8. John Barrymore		**h.**	*A Life of Her Own*
9. Lew Ayres		**i.**	*Bhowani Junction*
10. Paul Lukas		**j.**	*The Actress*

138. Of course, you can't ignore Great Kate for very long. Match the director to the Katharine Hepburn film he directed.

1. John Ford		**a.**	*Suddenly, Last Summer*
2. Gregory La Cava		**b.**	*State of the Union*
3. Frank Capra		**c.**	*The Sea of Grass*
4. Vincente Minnelli		**d.**	*Mary of Scotland*
5. David Lean		**e.**	*Woman of the Year*
6. Elia Kazan		**f.**	*Bringing Up Baby*
7. Joseph L. Mankiewicz		**g.**	*Undercurrent*
8. Howard Hawks		**h.**	*Pat and Mike*
9. George Cukor		**i.**	*Summertime*
10. George Stevens		**j.**	*Stage Door*

139. Match the director to the Gary Cooper film he directed.

1.	William A. Wellman	**a.**	*High Noon*
2.	Howard Hawks	**b.**	*The Fountainhead*
3.	Cecil B. DeMille	**c.**	*They Came to Cordura*
4.	Ernst Lubitsch	**d.**	*Friendly Persuasion*
5.	Sam Wood	**e.**	*Sergeant York*
6.	King Vidor	**f.**	*The Pride of the Yankees*
7.	Fred Zinnemann	**g.**	*Beau Geste*
8.	William Wyler	**h.**	*The Story of Dr. Wassell*
9.	Robert Rossen	**i.**	*Design for Living*
10.	Anthony Mann	**j.**	*Man of the West*

140. Match the director to the Marilyn Monroe film he directed.

1.	Henry Hathaway	**a.**	*River of No Return*
2.	Howard Hawks	**b.**	*Let's Make Love*
3.	Joseph L. Mankiewicz	**c.**	*Bus Stop*
4.	George Cukor	**d.**	*The Seven Year Itch*
5.	Billy Wilder	**e.**	*Monkey Business*
6.	Otto Preminger	**f.**	*How to Marry a Millionaire*
7.	Fritz Lang	**g.**	*The Asphalt Jungle*
8.	Joshua Logan	**h.**	*All About Eve*
9.	Jean Negulesco	**i.**	*Clash by Night*
10.	John Huston	**j.**	*Niagara*

141. Match the director to the John Wayne film he directed.

1.	John Ford	**a.**	*Sands of Iwo Jima*
2.	Howard Hawks	**b.**	*True Grit*
3.	John Wayne	**c.**	*Flying Leathernecks*
4.	Allan Dwan	**d.**	*The Barbarian and the Geisha*
5.	Dick Powell	**e.**	*In Harm's Way*
6.	Henry Hathaway	**f.**	*Rio Grande*
7.	John Huston	**g.**	*Rio Bravo*
8.	William A. Wellman	**h.**	*The Conqueror*
9.	Nicholas Ray	**i.**	*The Alamo*
10.	Otto Preminger	**j.**	*The High and the Mighty*

Barbara Stanwyck and Fred MacMurray in *Remember the Night*

THIRTEEN

"I Saw What You Did"

142. Match the occupational Rosalind Russell situation to the film in which it appears.

1.	She is a judge.	**a.**	*She Wouldn't Say Yes*
2.	She is an advertising executive.	**b.**	*His Girl Friday*
3.	She is a literary agent.	**c.**	*Design for Scandal*
4.	She is a psychiatrist.	**d.**	*A Woman of Distinction*
5.	She is a reporter.	**e.**	*Take a Letter, Darling*
6.	She is an aviatrix.	**f.**	*Picnic*
7.	She is an actress.	**g.**	*Flight for Freedom*
8.	She is a schoolteacher.	**h.**	*This Thing Called Love*
9.	She is a college dean.	**i.**	*What a Woman!*
10.	She is an insurance executive.	**j.**	*The Velvet Touch*

143. Match the light comic Cary Grant situation to the film in which it appears.

1. He is engaged to Julia, but ends up with her sister Linda.

    a. *The Bishop's Wife*

2. He must pretend to be Joseph the gardener.

    b. *Arsenic and Old Lace*

3. He announces that he just went gay all of a sudden.

    c. *Holiday*

4. His unearthly powers cause a bottle of sherry to be bottomless.

    d. *The Awful Truth*

5. His soon-to-be ex-wife embarrasses him by pretending to be his floozie sister Lola.

    e. *His Girl Friday*

6. He has been working for *Spy Magazine* ever since his divorce.

    f. *The Talk of the Town*

7. He gets some of his relatives admitted to Happy Dale.

    g. *My Favorite Wife*

8. He tries to come up with an ad slogan for a ham product.

    h. *The Philadelphia Story*

9. He describes his rival Bruce as looking like Ralph Bellamy (Bellamy plays Bruce).

    i. *Bringing Up Baby*

10. He is alarmed to learn that his wife was recently known as Eve to a hunk she called Adam.

    j. *Mr. Blandings Builds His Dream House*

144. Match the murderous Bette Davis situation to the film in which it appears.

1. She tries to kill her husband and/or herself in a car crash, but they both survive.

    a. *Dangerous*

2. She causes a large cement urn to fall and crush her cousin and a doctor.

    b. *The Letter*

3. She kills her cleaning woman with a hammer.

    c. *In This Our Life*

4. She kills a child in a hit-and-run accident.

    d. *The Little Foxes*

5. She shoots her lover six times on the front steps.

    e. *Hush . . . Hush, Sweet Charlotte*

6. She kills her twin.

    f. *Deception*

7. She kills a great composer (her former lover).

    g. *Beyond the Forest*

8. She causes her husband's death by refusing to bring him his medication.

    h. *What Ever Happened to Baby Jane?*

9. She uses a rifle to kill a man during a hunting trip.

    i. *All This, and Heaven Too*

10. She is imprisoned for complicity in a woman's murder, but is released for lack of evidence.

    j. *Dead Ringer*

145. Match the outlandish Jack Lemmon situation to the film in which it appears.

1. He goes to jail for the murder of his alter ego (Lord X).

    a. *The Odd Couple*

2. He causes a laundry disaster that buries him in suds.

    b. *The Apartment*

3. He chases (and ultimately rescues) an old woman in a speeding wheelchair.

    c. *The Great Race*

4. He drains spaghetti with a tennis racket.

    d. *Mister Roberts*

5. He confesses to his fiancé that he's not a natural blonde.

    e. *Irma La Douce*

6. He falls head first into a giant cake during a pie fight.

    f. *Bell, Book and Candle*

7. He and his ex-wife try to out-mambo each other at a nightclub.

    g. *Some Like It Hot*

8. His initials are F.U.

    h. *Under the Yum Yum Tree*

9. He is the bongo drum player at the Zodiac Club.

    i. *The Notorious Landlady*

10. He is the lecherous landlord of Centaur Apartments.

    j. *Phffft*

146. Match the unsavory Barbara Stanwyck situation to the film in which it appears.

1. She walks out on her family and winds up in third-rate vaudeville.

    a. *Double Indemnity*

2. She assumes the identity of a woman killed in a train wreck.

    b. *Baby Face*

3. She throws a pair of scissors into a woman's face.

    c. *California*

4. She tries to prevent her husband from leaving a burning house.

    d. *No Man of Her Own*

5. She and an insurance salesman carry out the murder of her husband.

    e. *All I Desire*

6. She encourages a man to kill her husband, who is unconscious at the foot of a long staircase.

    f. *Remember the Night*

7. She is literally thrown out of town by a group of upstanding women.

    g. *The Violent Men*

8. She steals an expensive bracelet from a jewelry store and is promptly arrested.

    h. *Clash by Night*

9. She sleeps her way to the top of the Gotham Trust Company.

    i. *The Furies*

10. She marries a gentle fisherman but has an affair with his volatile best friend.

    j. *The Strange Love of Martha Ivers*

147. Match the surprisingly dark James Stewart situation to the film in which it appears.

1. He contemplates suicide on a bridge during a snowstorm.

    a. *Vertigo*

2. He is a doctor wanted by the police for the mercy killing of his wife.

    b. *Bend of the River*

3. He is a bounty hunter passing himself off as a sheriff.

    c. *Rear Window*

4. He has scars on his neck from the time vigilantes tried to hang him.

    d. *It's a Wonderful Life*

5. He kills his brother for the murder of their father.

    e. *The Man from Laramie*

6. He is lassoed and dragged through a campfire.

    f. *The Naked Spur*

7. He loses a leg because of a hunting accident.

    g. *The Far Country*

8. He falls from a window moments after the police save him from a killer.

    h. *The Greatest Show on Earth*

9. He refuses the people of Dawson when they need him to be their marshal.

    i. *The Stratton Story*

10. He forces a brunette to become an exact replica of the blonde he loved and lost.

    j. *Winchester '73*

148. Match the amusing Claudette Colbert situation to the film in which it appears.

1. Her nightclub act is a triumph of personality over musical skills.

    a. *Without Reservations*

2. Despite her royal blood, she takes work as a housemaid.

    b. *The Palm Beach Story*

3. She is a poet who does some amateur sleuthing.

    c. *The Gilded Lily*

4. She is a novelist traveling to Hollywood by train.

    d. *Midnight*

5. She escapes her father by diving off his yacht.

    e. *It Happened One Night*

6. The Wienie King gets her out of debt.

    f. *Tovarich*

7. She purposely eats raw scallions to discourage her husband's amorous advances.

    g. *It's a Wonderful World*

8. She uses paint to write "I'm Through!" on a wall.

    h. *Arise, My Love*

9. She is stranded in Paris with nothing but her evening gown.

    i. *Bluebeard's Eighth Wife*

10. She pretends to be the wife of an imprisoned flyer.

    j. *The Egg and I*

149. Match the intense situation to the film about mental illness in which it appears.

1. A man throws a type-writer at his wife which smashes her hand.

    a. *Possessed* (1947)

2. A woman sits quietly in a boat as her brother-in-law drowns nearby.

    b. *A Bill of Divorcement*

3. A woman fears she has inherited her father's insanity and opts for celibacy.

    c. *Kings Row*

4. A woman wanders the streets of L.A. asking strangers for David.

    d. *Autumn Leaves*

5. A man cannot bear to see rows of lines on white backgrounds.

    e. *The Snake Pit*

6. A woman recalls a child-hood incident in which she was forced to kiss her dead grandmother good-bye.

    f. *Leave Her to Heaven*

7. A woman recalls a child-hood incident in which she wished her father would die and he did.

    g. *Suddenly, Last Summer*

8. A woman tries to secure an unnecessary lobotomy for her niece.

    h. *Spellbound*

9. A brilliant doctor poisons his troubled daughter and then shoots himself.

    i. *Fear Strikes Out*

10. A young man has a public breakdown due to pressure from his impossible-to-please father.

    j. *The Three Faces of Eve*

150. Smoking may be increasingly prohibited in American life, but can you imagine the movies without cigarettes? Match the cigarette-related event to the movie in which it appears.

1. A woman's cigarette is put out in a jar of cold cream.

   a. *Now, Voyager*

2. A woman's cigarette is put out in the yolk of a fried egg.

   b. *Strangers on a Train*

3. A woman's cigarette is put out in a nun's hand.

   c. *Smash-Up: The Story of a Woman*

4. A widow smokes from under her mourning veil.

   d. *Love Is a Many-Splendored Thing*

5. A lounge singer stains her piano by placing lit cigarettes on top of it whenever she plays.

   e. *Suddenly, Last Summer*

6. A woman's cigarette (in a very long holder) sets another woman's hat on fire.

   f. *Rebecca*

7. A man lights two cigarettes in his mouth (one is for Charlotte Vale).

   g. *Road House*

8. A woman's cigarette starts a bedroom fire that endangers her daughter.

   h. *Breakfast at Tiffany's*

9. A man uses his lit cigarette to pop a child's balloon at an amusement park.

   i. *To Catch a Thief*

10. A man lights his lover's cigarette by pressing the lit one in his mouth against the unlit one in hers.

    j. *Stage Fright*

151. Match the imaginative lipstick-related event to the film in which it appears.

1. A woman writes "No Sale" in lipstick on a mirror.

2. A woman uses lipstick to write her initials (C.P.) on a man's chest.

3. A woman uses lipstick to put a mustache on a movie mogul's plaque.

4. A woman throws an S.O.S. note written in lipstick out a skyscraper window.

5. A woman uses lipstick to write a message on the nightgown she is wearing and then throws herself out a window.

6. Lipstick stains on a cigarette butt provide a vital clue in an F.B.I. investigation.

7. A woman wipes off her lipstick using her bare hand and her feather boa.

8. A lipstick tube rolling on the floor marks the entrance of Cora.

9. A man uses lipstick to write the initials E.B. and N.M. (in a heart) on a backstage wall.

10. A woman uses lipstick to write her room number on a man's thigh.

a. *Destry Rides Again*

b. *Saboteur*

c. *The House on 92nd Street*

d. *On Her Majesty's Secret Service*

e. *Butterfield 8*

f. *The Bad and the Beautiful*

g. *Lifeboat*

h. *A Star Is Born* (1954)

i. *Three on a Match*

j. *The Postman Always Rings Twice* (1946)

Joan Crawford in *Sudden Fear*

FOURTEEN

"Author! Author!"

152. Match the playwright to the film for which he/she wrote the screenplay.

1.	Moss Hart	**a.**	*The Best Years of Our Lives*
2.	Garson Kanin	**b.**	*Gone With the Wind*
3.	Robert E. Sherwood	**c.**	*It Should Happen to You*
4.	Ben Hecht	**d.**	*The Manchurian Candidate*
5.	Paddy Chayefsky	**e.**	*Dead End*
6.	Lillian Hellman	**f.**	*A Star Is Born* (1954)
7.	Paul Osborn	**g.**	*The Goddess*
8.	Sidney Howard	**h.**	*Splendor in the Grass*
9.	William Inge	**i.**	*Notorious*
10.	George Axelrod	**j.**	*East of Eden*

153. Match the film on the left to the play or musical on the right that we see rehearsed and/or performed in the film (in one of them, we see only the curtain call).

1.	*Auntie Mame*	**a.**	*The Young Sarah*
2.	*All About Eve*	**b.**	*The Land Around Us*
3.	*The Country Girl*	**c.**	*Halfway to Heaven*
4.	*Stage Door*	**d.**	*Othello*
5.	*The Barkleys of Broadway*	**e.**	*Pretty Lady*
6.	*Twentieth Century*	**f.**	*Enchanted April*
7.	*A Double Life*	**g.**	*Midsummer Madness*
8.	*Dangerous*	**h.**	*But to Die*
9.	*Sudden Fear*	**i.**	*Aged in Wood*
10.	*42nd Street*	**j.**	*The Heart of Kentucky*

154. Match the writer to the film for which he/she wrote or co-wrote the screenplay.

1.	Aldous Huxley	**a.**	*Suddenly, Last Summer*
2.	Truman Capote	**b.**	*Easter Parade*
3.	Dorothy Parker	**c.**	*Beat the Devil*
4.	Sidney Sheldon	**d.**	*Moby Dick* (1956)
5.	John Steinbeck	**e.**	*To Have and Have Not*
6.	Gore Vidal	**f.**	*Pride and Prejudice*
7.	F. Scott Fitzgerald	**g.**	*The Night of the Hunter*
8.	William Faulkner	**h.**	*A Star Is Born* (1937)
9.	James Agee	**i.**	*Three Comrades*
10.	Ray Bradbury	**j.**	*Viva Zapata!*

155. Match the film on the left to the fictional book on the right that is written by a character in the film.

1. *Theodora Goes Wild*
2. *The Ghost and Mrs. Muir*
3. *Suspicion*
4. *Auntie Mame*
5. *Cluny Brown*
6. *The Bad and the Beautiful*
7. *Arsenic and Old Lace*
8. *Spellbound*
9. *The Seven Year Itch*
10. *Old Acquaintance*

a. *The Nightingale Murder!*
b. *The Sinner*
c. *Of Man and the Unconscious*
d. *Blood and Swash*
e. *Marriage, a Fraud and a Failure*
f. *Labyrinth of the Guilt Complex*
g. *Murder on the Footbridge*
h. *Married in June*
i. *Live! Live! Live!*
j. *A Woman of Taste*

156. Match the star to his/her autobiography.

1. Gene Tierney
2. Alec Guinness
3. Joan Fontaine
4. Joseph Cotten
5. Katharine Hepburn
6. Dirk Bogarde
7. Bette Davis
8. Mary Astor
9. Lilli Palmer
10. Janet Leigh

a. *Vanity Will Get You Somewhere*
b. *Change Lobsters and Dance*
c. *The Lonely Life*
d. *Blessings in Disguise*
e. *Snakes & Ladders*
f. *There Really Was a Hollywood*
g. *Self-Portrait*
h. *A Life on Film*
i. *No Bed of Roses*
j. *Me*

Spencer Tracy and Clark Gable in *Test Pilot*

FIFTEEN

"Man Hunt"

Hint. Again, each star has 5 correct answers.

157. Charlie Chaplin or Buster Keaton?

1. Who directed the 1923 drama *A Woman of Paris?*
2. Who was a Best Actor nominee at the first Academy Awards?
3. Who appeared in *Around the World in Eighty Days?*
4. Who was under contract to MGM?
5. Who appeared as himself in the 1928 Marion Davies comedy *Show People?*
6. Who won a N.Y. Film Critics Award for acting?
7. Whose *Three Ages* was a spoof of *Intolerance?*
8. Who appeared in the all-star *The Hollywood Revue of 1929?*
9. Who directed and appeared with Martha Raye in a 1947 film?
10. Who made a cameo appearance in *Sunset Boulevard?*

158. Humphrey Bogart or Edward G. Robinson?

  1. Who won a Best Actor Oscar?

  2. Who received a posthumous honorary Oscar?

  3. Who starred in *The Return of Dr. X*?

  4. Who recreated a stage triumph in a 1936 film?

  5. Who starred in two Fritz Lang films?

  6. Who starred in a film directed by Orson Welles?

  7. Who starred with Barbara Stanwyck in *The Violent Men*?

  8. Who starred with June Allyson in *Battle Circus*?

  9. Who dies at the end of *Key Largo*?

 10. Who appeared in two William Wyler films?

159. Clark Gable or Spencer Tracy?

  1. Who dies at the end of *Test Pilot*?

  2. Who marries Claudette Colbert in *Boom Town*?

  3. Whose last film was directed by John Huston?

  4. Who starred with Garbo in *Susan Lenox (Her Fall and Rise)*?

  5. Who teamed with Rosalind Russell in *They Met in Bombay*?

  6. Who teamed with Joan Crawford in *Mannequin*?

  7. Who was Oscar-nominated for *San Francisco*?

  8. Who starred in a western directed by Elia Kazan?

  9. Who joined Myrna Loy and William Powell in *Libeled Lady*?

 10. Who joined Myrna Loy and William Powell in *Manhattan Melodrama*?

160. Cary Grant or James Stewart?

1. Who starred in a remake of the silent *Seventh Heaven*?
2. Who made two films with Ginger Rogers?
3. Who marries Katharine Hepburn at the end of *The Philadelphia Story*?
4. Who starred with Joan Crawford in *The Ice Follies of 1939*?
5. Who starred with Deborah Kerr in *Dream Wife*?
6. Who appeared in one of the Jeanette MacDonald/Nelson Eddy operettas?
7. Who played Roger Thornhill in a Hitchcock thriller?
8. Who teamed with Rosalind Russell in *No Time for Comedy*?
9. Who played the male lead in the musical extravaganza *Ziegfeld Girl*?
10. Who played Leopold Dilg in a 1942 Oscar nominee for Best Picture?

161. Errol Flynn or Tyrone Power?

1. Who played Jake Barnes in *The Sun Also Rises*?
2. Who starred in *Prince of Foxes* and *Son of Fury*?
3. Who starred in *Virginia City* and *San Antonio*?
4. Who fought World War II in *Desperate Journey*?
5. Who fought World War II in *Crash Dive*?
6. Who starred with Maureen O'Hara in *The Black Swan*?
7. Who starred with Maureen O'Hara in *Against All Flags*?
8. Who played Greer Garson's husband in *That Forsyte Woman*?
9. Who starred in Rudyard Kipling's *Kim* with Dean Stockwell?
10. Who was replaced by Yul Brynner when he died during the filming of *Solomon and Sheba*?

162. Joel McCrea or Randolph Scott?

1. Who starred in a western remake of *High Sierra*?
2. Who appeared in two musicals with Fred Astaire?
3. Who starred with Helen Gahagan in the 1935 camp classic *She*?
4. Who romanced Jean Arthur in *The More the Merrier*?
5. Who starred as *Buffalo Bill*, *The Virginian* and Wyatt Earp in *Wichita*?
6. Who made two films with Marlene Dietrich in 1942?
7. Who starred in Alfred Hitchcock's *Foreign Correspondent*?
8. Who got caught between Irene Dunne and Cary Grant in *My Favorite Wife*?
9. Who starred with Barbara Stanwyck in DeMille's *Union Pacific*?
10. Who played Gil Westrum in *Ride the High Country*?

163. Fred Astaire or Gene Kelly?

1. Who starred in the modest musical *Living in a Big Way*?
2. Who starred in a musical directed by George Cukor?
3. Who starred in a musical directed by Francis Ford Coppola?
4. Who paired with June Allyson in a 1948 film?
5. Who was the first to star in a Vincente Minnelli musical?
6. Who introduced an Oscar-winning song?
7. Whose first film was directed by Busby Berkeley?
8. Who was in Stanley Donen's first solo directorial effort?
9. Who danced in a Roland Petit ballet with Leslie Caron in a 1955 musical?
10. Who made a cameo in the Marilyn Monroe musical *Let's Make Love*?

164. Alec Guinness or Laurence Olivier?

1. Who appeared with Irene Dunne in *The Mudlark*?
2. Who had a featured role in *Doctor Zhivago*?
3. Who starred with Simone Signoret in *Term of Trial*?
4. Who teamed with John Mills in *Tunes of Glory*?
5. Who appeared with Bette Davis in *The Scapegoat*?
6. Who played The Mahdi in *Khartoum* with Charlton Heston?
7. Who played the inspector in *Bunny Lake Is Missing*?
8. Who played Sophia Loren's father in *The Fall of the Roman Empire*?
9. Who found Tony Curtis irresistible in the restored version of a 1960 epic?
10. Who appeared with Kirk Douglas and Burt Lancaster in *The Devil's Disciple*?

165. Kirk Douglas or Burt Lancaster?

1. Who starred in a 1951 Billy Wilder drama with Jan Sterling?
2. Who made films with Tony Curtis in 1956 and 1957?
3. Who played the villain in *Seven Days in May*?
4. Whose first film starred Barbara Stanwyck?
5. Who appeared with Rosalind Russell in *Mourning Becomes Electra*?
6. Who starred in three Vincente Minnelli films?
7. Who won a Best Actor Oscar?
8. Who starred with Audrey Hepburn in a 1960 western?
9. Who starred with Gary Cooper in the 1954 western *Vera Cruz*?
10. Who played Doc Holliday in *Gunfight at the O.K. Corral*?

166. Marlon Brando or Montgomery Clift?

1. Who starred in a 1954 Vittorio De Sica film?
2. Who starred with Sophia Loren in a film directed by Charlie Chaplin?
3. Who starred in an Alfred Hitchcock film?
4. Who starred in a Howard Hawks western?
5. Who made his screen debut opposite Teresa Wright?
6. Who starred in a comedy with Shirley Jones?
7. Who starred in the 1953 Oscar-winning Best Picture?
8. Who starred in the 1954 Oscar-winning Best Picture?
9. Who appeared in a 1961 film with an original screenplay by Arthur Miller?
10. Who played Christian Diestl in *The Young Lions*?

Rita Hayworth and Fred Astaire in *You Were Never Lovelier*

SIXTEEN

"Let's Dance"

167. Match the dancer or dancing team to the musical in which he/she/they performed.

1.	The Nicholas Brothers	**a.**	*Li'l Abner*
2.	Bob Fosse	**b.**	*Les Girls*
3.	Marge and Gower Champion	**c.**	*Hit the Deck* (1955)
4.	Vera-Ellen	**d.**	*The Pirate*
5.	Cyd Charisse	**e.**	*April in Paris*
6.	Mitzi Gaynor	**f.**	*Damn Yankees*
7.	Julie Newmar	**g.**	*Call Me Madam*
8.	Ray Bolger	**h.**	*Singin' in the Rain*
9.	James Cagney	**i.**	*Lovely to Look At*
10.	Russ Tamblyn	**j.**	*The Seven Little Foys*

168. Match the remarkable (and sometimes groundbreaking) dance sequence to the musical in which it appears.

1. "From This Moment On"
2. "Girl Hunt"
3. "Swingin' the Jinx Away"
4. "Frankie and Johnny"
5. "Slaughter on 10th Avenue"
6. "Limehouse Blues"
7. "Let's Say It with Firecrackers"
8. "You're All the World to Me"
9. "The Barn-Raising Dance"
10. "Steppin' Out With My Baby"

a. *Born to Dance*
b. *Ziegfeld Follies*
c. *Kiss Me Kate*
d. *Words and Music*
e. *Easter Parade*
f. *Royal Wedding*
g. *Meet Me in Las Vegas*
h. *The Band Wagon*
i. *Holiday Inn*
j. *Seven Brides for Seven Brothers*

169. Match the choreographer to the musical for which he/she created the dances. In some of these instances, the choreographers adapted work they had originated on Broadway.

1. Bob Fosse
2. Michael Kidd
3. Agnes de Mille
4. Gene Kelly
5. Roland Petit
6. Jack Cole
7. Hermes Pan
8. Jerome Robbins
9. Onna White
10. Robert Alton

a. *The Band Wagon*
b. *Brigadoon*
c. *The Pajama Game*
d. *Top Hat*
e. *Gentlemen Prefer Blondes*
f. *Easter Parade*
g. *Oliver!*
h. *Oklahoma!*
i. *The King and I*
j. *Hans Christian Andersen*

170. Match the Fred Astaire dance number to the woman who was his partner. Then name the film.

1.	"Heigh Ho, the Gang's All Here"	**a.**	Ginger Rogers
2.	"Begin the Beguine"	**b.**	Lucille Bremer
3.	"This Heart of Mine"	**c.**	Eleanor Powell
4.	"It Only Happens When I Dance with You"	**d.**	Leslie Caron
5.	"I'm Old-Fashioned"	**e.**	Audrey Hepburn
6.	"Pick Yourself Up"		
7.	"Something's Gotta Give"	**f.**	Joan Crawford
8.	"I Left My Hat in Haiti"	**g.**	Jane Powell
9.	"All of You"	**h.**	Cyd Charisse
10.	"He Loves and She Loves"	**i.**	Rita Hayworth
		j.	Ann Miller

171. Match the male performer to the musical number in which he danced (or at least moved well) with Gene Kelly. Then name the film.

1.	Frank Sinatra	**a.**	"I Begged Her"
2.	Van Johnson	**b.**	"Make Way for Tomorrow"
3.	Phil Silvers	**c.**	"The Worry Song"
4.	Donald O'Connor	**d.**	"The Babbitt and the Bromide"
5.	Dan Dailey	**e.**	"Moses Supposes"
6.	Georges Guetary	**f.**	"The Alter Ego Dance"
7.	Fred Kelly (his brother)	**g.**	"March, March"
8.	Fred Astaire	**h.**	" 'S Wonderful"
9.	Jerry the Mouse	**i.**	"I'll Go Home with Bonnie Jean"
10.	Gene Kelly	**j.**	"I Love to Go Swimmin' with Women"

Fredric March and Constance Bennett in *The Affairs of Cellini*

SEVENTEEN

"Oh, Men! Oh, Women!"

172. Match the actress to the film in which she appeared with either Fredric March or William Powell.

1. Esther Williams
2. Joan Bennett
3. Jean Harlow
4. Ann Blyth
5. Fay Wray
6. Bette Davis
7. Hedy Lamarr
8. Norma Shearer
9. Miriam Hopkins
10. Merle Oberon

a. *Dr. Jekyll and Mr. Hyde* with Fredric March
b. *Fashions of 1934* with William Powell
c. *The Affairs of Cellini* with Fredric March
d. *The Heavenly Body* with William Powell
e. *Trade Winds* with Fredric March
f. *The Hoodlum Saint* with William Powell
g. *Smilin' Through* with Fredric March
h. *Reckless* with William Powell
i. *The Dark Angel* with Fredric March
j. *Mr. Peabody and the Mermaid* with William Powell

173. Match the actor to the film in which he appeared with either Susan Hayward or Gene Tierney.

1. Clark Gable	**a.** *Ada* with Susan Hayward
2. Henry Fonda	**b.** *Plymouth Adventure* with Gene Tierney
3. Tyrone Power	**c.** *White Witch Doctor* with Susan Hayward
4. Spencer Tracy	**d.** *The Left Hand of God* with Gene Tierney
5. Gary Cooper	**e.** *Untamed* with Susan Hayward
6. Dean Martin	**f.** *Never Let Me Go* with Gene Tierney
7. Humphrey Bogart	**g.** *The President's Lady* with Susan Hayward
8. Robert Mitchum	**h.** *Rings on Her Fingers* with Gene Tierney
9. Dana Andrews	**i.** *Garden of Evil* with Susan Hayward
10. Charlton Heston	**j.** *The Iron Curtain* with Gene Tierney

174. Match the actress to the film in which she appeared with either Fred MacMurray or Ray Milland.

1. Jean Arthur	**a.** *The Lady Is Willing* with Fred MacMurray
2. Claudette Colbert	**b.** *Kitty* with Ray Milland
3. Barbara Stanwyck	**c.** *Above Suspicion* with Fred MacMurray
4. Loretta Young	**d.** *Copper Canyon* with Ray Milland
5. Marlene Dietrich	**e.** *There's Always Tomorrow* with Fred MacMurray
6. Carole Lombard	**f.** *Easy Living* with Ray Milland
7. Irene Dunne	**g.** *Hands Across the Table* with Fred MacMurray
8. Hedy Lamarr	**h.** *The Doctor Takes a Wife* with Ray Milland
9. Paulette Goddard	**i.** *Never a Dull Moment* with Fred MacMurray
10. Joan Crawford	**j.** *Skylark* with Ray Milland

175. Match the actor to the film in which he appeared with either Lauren Bacall or Rita Hayworth.

1.	Richard Widmark	**a.**	*How to Marry a Millionaire* with Lauren Bacall
2.	William Powell	**b.**	*My Gal Sal* with Rita Hayworth
3.	Glenn Ford	**c.**	*Blood Alley* with Lauren Bacall
4.	Gary Cooper	**d.**	*Salome* with Rita Hayworth
5.	Burt Lancaster	**e.**	*Woman's World* with Lauren Bacall
6.	Victor Mature	**f.**	*The Loves of Carmen* with Rita Hayworth
7.	Fred MacMurray	**g.**	*The Cobweb* with Lauren Bacall
8.	Stewart Granger	**h.**	*Fire Down Below* with Rita Hayworth
9.	Robert Mitchum	**i.**	*Bright Leaf* with Lauren Bacall
10.	John Wayne	**j.**	*Separate Tables* with Rita Hayworth

176. Match the actress to the film in which she appeared with either Alan Ladd or Robert Mitchum.

1.	Dorothy Lamour	**a.**	*Salty O'Rourke* with Alan Ladd
2.	Linda Darnell	**b.**	*Home from the Hill* with Robert Mitchum
3.	Janet Leigh	**c.**	*China* with Alan Ladd
4.	Geraldine Fitzgerald	**d.**	*Second Chance* with Robert Mitchum
5.	Loretta Young	**e.**	*Wild Harvest* with Alan Ladd
6.	Shelley Winters	**f.**	*Not As a Stranger* with Robert Mitchum
7.	Gail Russell	**g.**	*O.S.S.* with Alan Ladd
8.	Eleanor Parker	**h.**	*The Night of the Hunter* with Robert Mitchum
9.	Virginia Mayo	**i.**	*The Iron Mistress* with Alan Ladd
10.	Olivia de Havilland	**j.**	*Holiday Affair* with Robert Mitchum

177. Match the actor to the film in which he appeared with either Jennifer Jones or Deborah Kerr.

1. John Garfield	**a.**	*Madame Bovary* with Jennifer Jones
2. Gary Cooper	**b.**	*Edward, My Son* with Deborah Kerr
3. Charles Boyer	**c.**	*We Were Strangers* with Jennifer Jones
4. David Niven	**d.**	*The Hucksters* with Deborah Kerr
5. Spencer Tracy	**e.**	*Indiscretion of an American Wife* with Jennifer Jones
6. Montgomery Clift	**f.**	*The Naked Edge* with Deborah Kerr
7. William Eythe	**g.**	*Cluny Brown* with Jennifer Jones
8. Yul Brynner	**h.**	*The Journey* with Deborah Kerr
9. Louis Jourdan	**i.**	*The Song of Bernadette* with Jennifer Jones
10. Clark Gable	**j.**	*Bonjour Tristesse* with Deborah Kerr

Clifton Webb and Gene Tierney in *Laura*

EIGHTEEN

"The Professionals"

178. Have you been paying attention to the opening credits? Match the film industry employee to his/her skill.

1. Sydney Guilaroff	**a.** producing
2. Natalie Kalmus	**b.** screenwriting
3. Margaret Booth	**c.** cinematography
4. Harry Stradling	**d.** art direction
5. Dorothy Jeakins	**e.** film editing
6. Douglas Shearer	**f.** costume design
7. Franz Waxman	**g.** composing scores
8. Dalton Trumbo	**h.** Technicolor color direction
9. Pandro S. Berman	**i.** hair styling
10. Cedric Gibbons	**j.** sound recording

179. 1939 is usually regarded as Hollywood's peak. Let us give some of the credit where credit is due . . . in the credits. Match the '39 classic to its corresponding credit.

1. *The Women*		**a.**	Produced by Mervyn LeRoy
2. *Gunga Din*		**b.**	Co-written by Billy Wilder
3. *Ninotchka*		**c.**	Lyrics by Frank Loesser
4. *Of Mice and Men*		**d.**	Directed by George Stevens
5. *Destry Rides Again*		**e.**	Produced by Samuel Goldwyn
6. *Wuthering Heights*		**f.**	Featuring Rita Hayworth
7. *The Wizard of Oz*		**g.**	Featuring Paulette Goddard
8. *Only Angels Have Wings*		**h.**	Screenplay by Dudley Nichols
9. *Stagecoach*		**i.**	Directed by Lewis Milestone
10. *Gone With the Wind*		**j.**	Photographed by Ernest Haller

180. Match the acclaimed film to its great cinematographer.

1. *Citizen Kane*		**a.**	Stanley Cortez
2. *Touch of Evil*		**b.**	James Wong Howe
3. *Vertigo*		**c.**	Russell Metty
4. *Queen Christina*		**d.**	Burnett Guffey
5. *Casablanca*		**e.**	Gregg Toland
6. *The Magnificent Ambersons*		**f.**	William Daniels
7. *From Here to Eternity*		**g.**	Jack Cardiff
8. *The Searchers*		**h.**	Arthur Edeson
9. *The African Queen*		**i.**	Robert Burks
10. *Hud*		**j.**	Winton C. Hoch

181. Here's one for those of you who get excited by a "Gowns by . . ." credit. Match the memorably costumed film to its celebrated designer.

1.	*Gone With the Wind*	**a.**	Adrian
2.	*The Wizard of Oz*	**b.**	Helen Rose
3.	*Gigi*	**c.**	Irene Sharaff
4.	*Gilda*	**d.**	Orry-Kelly
5.	*The Scarlet Empress*	**e.**	Travilla
6.	*A Place in the Sun*	**f.**	Jean Louis
7.	*The Bad and the Beautiful*	**g.**	Walter Plunkett
8.	*The King and I*	**h.**	Travis Banton
9.	*Auntie Mame*	**i.**	Edith Head
10.	*Gentlemen Prefer Blondes*	**j.**	Cecil Beaton

182. Match the composer to the film for which he wrote the score.

1.	Leonard Bernstein	**a.**	*The Heiress*
2.	Max Steiner	**b.**	*The High and the Mighty*
3.	Aaron Copland	**c.**	*Anatomy of a Murder*
4.	David Raksin	**d.**	*Laura*
5.	Erich Wolfgang Korngold	**e.**	*Citizen Kane*
6.	Bernard Herrmann	**f.**	*On the Waterfront*
7.	Dimitri Tiomkin	**g.**	*Kings Row*
8.	Ernest Gold	**h.**	*Spellbound*
9.	Duke Ellington	**i.**	*Now, Voyager*
10.	Miklós Rózsa	**j.**	*Exodus*

James Mason in *Five Fingers*

NINETEEN

"Change of Habit"

183. Match the musical performer to the film in which he/she played a dramatic role.

1. Judy Garland	**a.** *Christmas Holiday*
2. Esther Williams	**b.** *Little Boy Lost*
3. Debbie Reynolds	**c.** *A Child Is Waiting*
4. Dick Powell	**d.** *Cornered*
5. Bing Crosby	**e.** *I Wake Up Screaming*
6. Betty Grable	**f.** *The Catered Affair*
7. Gene Kelly	**g.** *The Young Lions*
8. Doris Day	**h.** *Storm Warning*
9. Dean Martin	**i.** *Twilight for the Gods*
10. Cyd Charisse	**j.** *The Unguarded Moment*

184. Match the usually nonmusical performer to the musical in which he/she sang and/or danced (sometimes rather well and sometimes blessedly briefly).

1. Claudette Colbert	**a.** *The Harvey Girls*
2. Louis Calhern	**b.** *Broadway Melody of 1936*
3. Arlene Dahl	**c.** *The Smiling Lieutenant*
4. Walter Huston	**d.** *Silk Stockings*
5. Paulette Goddard	**e.** *Call Me Madam*
6. Robert Taylor	**f.** *Second Chorus*
7. Marjorie Main	**g.** *Annie Get Your Gun*
8. George Sanders	**h.** *Les Girls*
9. Kay Kendall	**i.** *Yankee Doodle Dandy*
10. Peter Lorre	**j.** *Three Little Words*

185. Match the silent star to the talking picture in which he/she played a supporting role.

1. Lillian Gish	**a.** *In the Good Old Summertime*
2. Richard Barthelmess	**b.** *The Unforgiven*
3. Dolores Costello	**c.** *Since You Went Away*
4. Buster Keaton	**d.** *Only Angels Have Wings*
5. Alla Nazimova	**e.** *The Searchers*
6. Conrad Nagel	**f.** *Sabrina* (1954)
7. Jackie Coogan	**g.** *The Magnificent Ambersons*
8. Ramon Novarro	**h.** *Heller in Pink Tights*
9. Antonio Moreno	**i.** *The Joker Is Wild*
10. Francis X. Bushman	**j.** *All That Heaven Allows*

186. Match the television star to the film in which he/she appeared before fame hit on the small screen.

1.	Ted Knight	**a.**	*Cleopatra* (1963)
2.	Carroll O'Connor	**b.**	*On the Waterfront*
3.	Cloris Leachman	**c.**	*The Treasure of the Sierra Madre*
4.	June Lockhart	**d.**	*Psycho*
5.	George Reeves	**e.**	*Twelve Angry Men*
6.	Robert Blake	**f.**	*Meet Me in St. Louis*
7.	Jack Klugman	**g.**	*A Place in the Sun*
8.	Jack Webb	**h.**	*Gone With the Wind*
9.	Fred Gwynne	**i.**	*Kiss Me Deadly*
10.	Raymond Burr	**j.**	*Sunset Boulevard*

187. Match the Hollywood performer to the European film in which he/she appeared.

1.	Burt Lancaster	**a.**	*La Strada*
2.	Jean Seberg	**b.**	*Il Grido*
3.	Farley Granger	**c.**	*Elena et les Hommes*
4.	George Sanders	**d.**	*Breathless*
5.	Lex Barker	**e.**	*Contempt*
6.	Steve Cochran	**f.**	*Viaggio in Italia*
7.	Jack Palance	**g.**	*Diary of a Lost Girl*
8.	Mel Ferrer	**h.**	*Senso*
9.	Richard Basehart	**i.**	*The Leopard*
10.	Louise Brooks	**j.**	*La Dolce Vita*

188. Match the international star to the American film in which he/she appeared.

1. Anna Magnani	**a.** *Ship of Fools*
2. Max von Sydow	**b.** *The Train*
3. Simone Signoret	**c.** *My Geisha*
4. Toshiro Mifune	**d.** *Five Fingers*
5. Danielle Darrieux	**e.** *All That Money Can Buy*
6. Cantinflas	**f.** *Hell in the Pacific*
7. Jeanne Moreau	**g.** *Hawaii*
8. Yves Montand	**h.** *Rhapsody*
9. Vittorio Gassman	**i.** *Pepe*
10. Simone Simon	**j.** *Wild Is the Wind*

189. Match the film professional (primarily known for something other than writing) to the film for which he/she wrote or contributed to the story and/or screenplay.

1. Frank Capra	**a.** *Since You Went Away*
2. Rosalind Russell	**b.** *Thunder Road*
3. Robert Mitchum	**c.** *The Horse's Mouth*
4. David O. Selznick	**d.** *Adam's Rib*
5. Burgess Meredith	**e.** *Monsieur Verdoux*
6. Ruth Gordon	**f.** *The Unguarded Moment*
7. Alec Guinness	**g.** *Private Hell 36*
8. Ida Lupino	**h.** *Take Me Out to the Ball Game*
9. Stanley Donen	**i.** *Westward the Women*
10. Orson Welles	**j.** *The Diary of a Chambermaid* (1946)

190. Match the performer to the film he/she directed.

1.	Gower Champion	a.	*The Enemy Below*
2.	Peter Ustinov	b.	*The Gallant Hours*
3.	Ida Lupino	c.	*The Man on the Eiffel Tower*
4.	Gene Kelly	d.	*Hello, Dolly!*
5.	Burgess Meredith	e.	*My Six Loves*
6.	Gene Nelson	f.	*State Fair* (1962)
7.	Robert Montgomery	g.	*Billy Budd*
8.	Dick Powell	h.	*The Buccaneer* (1958)
9.	Jose Ferrer	i.	*The Hitch-Hiker*
10.	Anthony Quinn	j.	*Harum Scarum*

191. Match the director or choreographer to the film in which he appeared in an acting role.

1.	Gregory Ratoff	a.	*It's Always Fair Weather*
2.	Vittorio De Sica	b.	*Five Graves to Cairo*
3.	John Huston	c.	*A Farewell to Arms* (1957)
4.	Michael Kidd	d.	*Never on Sunday*
5.	Preston Sturges	e.	*Stalag 17*
6.	Jules Dassin	f.	*Hold Back the Dawn*
7.	Jack Cole	g.	*All About Eve*
8.	Erich von Stroheim	h.	*Paris Holiday*
9.	Otto Preminger	i.	*The Cardinal*
10.	Mitchell Leisen	j.	*Designing Woman*

192. Match the usually nonmusical director to the musical film he directed.

1.	Henry King	**a.**	*Swing Time*
2.	William Wyler	**b.**	*Gentlemen Prefer Blondes*
3.	Fred Zinnemann	**c.**	*Show Boat* (1936)
4.	Howard Hawks	**d.**	*Funny Girl*
5.	Michael Curtiz	**e.**	*Guys and Dolls*
6.	George Stevens	**f.**	*Mary Poppins*
7.	Joseph L. Mankiewicz	**g.**	*Carousel*
8.	Otto Preminger	**h.**	*White Christmas*
9.	James Whale	**i.**	*Oklahoma!*
10.	Robert Stevenson	**j.**	*Carmen Jones*

193. Match the director (most often associated with musicals) to one of the nonmusical films he directed.

1. Vincente Minnelli	**a.** *The Three Musketeers* (1948)
2. Busby Berkeley	**b.** *Desk Set*
3. Rouben Mamoulian	**c.** *The Long, Long Trailer*
4. Roy Del Ruth	**d.** *The Tender Trap*
5. Stanley Donen	**e.** *So Proudly We Hail!*
6. Irving Cummings	**f.** *The Maltese Falcon* (1931)
7. George Sidney	**g.** *They Made Me a Criminal*
8. Charles Walters	**h.** *Golden Boy*
9. Mark Sandrich	**i.** *The Story of Alexander Graham Bell*
10. Walter Lang	**j.** *Charade*

Joel McCrea and Veronica Lake in *Sullivan's Travels*

TWENTY

"Stardust Memories"

194. Match the actor on the left to the movie star he played in a film.

1.	Rod Steiger	**a.**	Al Jolson
2.	James Cagney	**b.**	Eddie Cantor
3.	Kevin Kline	**c.**	Lon Chaney
4.	Larry Parks	**d.**	George Raft
5.	Errol Flynn	**e.**	Bela Lugosi
6.	Ray Danton	**f.**	W. C. Fields
7.	Donald O'Connor	**g.**	John Barrymore
8.	Keefe Brasselle	**h.**	Douglas Fairbanks
9.	Martin Landau	**i.**	Clark Gable
10.	James Brolin	**j.**	Buster Keaton

195. Pick the star's one black-and-white film in each group.

  1. Errol Flynn

    a. *Dive Bomber;*
    b. *Adventures of Don Juan;*
    c. *The Sea Hawk;* **d.** *Dodge City*

  2. Ingrid Bergman

    a. *Joan of Arc;* **b.** *Saratoga Trunk;*
    c. *Anastasia;* **d.** *Indiscreet*

  3. James Stewart

    a. *Winchester '73;* **b.** *Broken Arrow;*
    c. *The Naked Spur;*
    d. *Two Rode Together*

  4. Rita Hayworth

    a. *My Gal Sal;* **b.** *Fire Down Below;*
    c. *The Loves of Carmen;*
    d. *Affair in Trinidad*

  5. Gary Cooper

    a. *North West Mounted Police;*
    b. *Unconquered;*
    c. *The Adventures of Marco Polo;*
    d. *Friendly Persuasion*

  6. Susan Hayward

    a. *The Lusty Men;*
    b. *With a Song in My Heart;*
    c. *Canyon Passage;*
    d. *Soldier of Fortune*

  7. John Wayne

    a. *Hondo;* **b.** *The Horse Soldiers;*
    c. *Rio Bravo;* **d.** *Rio Grande*

  8. Audrey Hepburn

    a. *Green Mansions;*
    b. *Love in the Afternoon;* **c.** *Charade;*
    d. *The Nun's Story*

  9. Nelson Eddy

    a. *Sweethearts;* **b.** *Maytime;*
    c. *Bitter Sweet;*
    d. *The Phantom of the Opera*

 10. Deborah Kerr

    a. *The Sundowners;*
    b. *Heaven Knows, Mr. Allison;*
    c. *Separate Tables;*
    d. *The Grass Is Greener*

196. Pick the star's one color film in each group.

1. Robert Taylor   **a.** *Broadway Melody of 1938;*
   b. *Bataan;*   **c.** *Billy the Kid;*
   d. *The Gorgeous Hussy*

2. Alice Faye   **a.** *That Night in Rio;*
   b. *Lillian Russell;*   **c.** *Tin Pan Alley;*
   d. *In Old Chicago*

3. Tyrone Power   **a.** *The Mark of Zorro;*
   b. *Marie Antoinette;*
   c. *Lloyds of London;*   **d.** *Jesse James*

4. Marlene Dietrich   **a.** *The Flame of New Orleans;*
   b. *Kismet;*   **c.** *Golden Earrings;*
   d. *Stage Fright*

5. Fred Astaire   **a.** *Broadway Melody of 1940;*
   b. *Holiday Inn;*
   c. *You Were Never Lovelier;*
   d. *Blue Skies*

6. Greer Garson   **a.** *Random Harvest;*
   b. *Pride and Prejudice;*
   c. *Blossoms in the Dust;*
   d. *Julius Caesar*

7. Spencer Tracy   **a.** *Northwest Passage;*
   b. *Stanley and Livingstone;*
   c. *Captains Courageous;*
   d. *Boom Town*

8. Gene Tierney   **a.** *Dragonwyck;*
   b. *Leave Her to Heaven;*
   c. *The Mating Season;*
   d. *Advise and Consent*

9. William Holden   **a.** *Dear Ruth;*   **b.** *Executive Suite;*
   c. *The Moon Is Blue;*
   d. *Apartment for Peggy*

10. Carole Lombard   **a.** *Bolero;*
    b. *The Princess Comes Across;*
    c. *Nothing Sacred;*
    d. *Mr. and Mrs. Smith*

197. Pick the one film in each group in which the performer did not appear.

1. Betty Grable
   a. *Down Argentine Way;*
   b. *Week-End in Havana;*
   c. *Song of the Islands;*
   d. *Moon Over Miami*

2. Shirley Temple
   a. *Little Miss Broadway;*
   b. *Poor Little Rich Girl;*
   c. *The Littlest Rebel;*
   d. *Little Fugitive*

3. Eleanor Powell
   a. *Broadway Melody of 1936;*
   b. *Broadway Melody of 1938;*
   c. *Broadway Melody of 1940;*
   d. *Broadway Rhythm*

4. Dick Powell
   a. *The Goldwyn Follies;*
   b. *Gold Diggers of 1933;*
   c. *Gold Diggers of 1935;*
   d. *Gold Diggers of 1937*

5. Jean Harlow
   a. *Red-Headed Woman;* b. *Goldie;*
   c. *Blonde Crazy;* d. *Platinum Blonde*

6. Judy Garland
   a. *Andy Hardy Gets Spring Fever;*
   b. *Love Finds Andy Hardy;*
   c. *Andy Hardy Meets Debutante;*
   d. *Life Begins for Andy Hardy*

7. Claudette Colbert
   a. *Bride for Sale;*
   b. *The Bride Comes Home;*
   c. *The Bride Goes Wild;* d. *Guest Wife*

8. Kirk Douglas
   a. *The Big Land;* b. *The Big Sky;*
   c. *The Big Trees;* d. *The Last Sunset*

9. Esther Williams
   a. *The Duchess of Idaho;*
   b. *Texas Carnival;*
   c. *Sun Valley Serenade;* d. *Fiesta*

10. Doris Day
    a. *Tea for Two;*
    b. *The Best Things in Life Are Free;*
    c. *Lullaby of Broadway;*
    d. *My Dream Is Yours*

198. Sometimes big stars make surprise appearances. Match the star to the film in which he/she makes a cameo.

1. Joan Crawford		**a.**	*Till the Clouds Roll By*
2. Bing Crosby		**b.**	*Three Sailors and a Girl*
3. Robert Taylor		**c.**	*Without Reservations*
4. Myrna Loy		**d.**	*The Princess and the Pirate*
5. Esther Williams		**e.**	*The Band Wagon*
6. Ava Gardner		**f.**	*It's a Great Feeling*
7. Burt Lancaster		**g.**	*Paris When It Sizzles*
8. Cary Grant		**h.**	*I Love Melvin*
9. Veronica Lake		**i.**	*The Senator Was Indiscreet*
10. Marlene Dietrich		**j.**	*Hold Back the Dawn*

199. People often go to the movies in movies. One of the films on the right is watched in one of the films on the left. Match them.

1. *Bonnie and Clyde*		**a.**	*Top Hat*
2. *Get Shorty*		**b.**	*Duck Soup*
3. *Summer of '42*		**c.**	*Roman Holiday*
4. *Radio Days*		**d.**	*Vertigo*
5. *Words and Music*		**e.**	*Follow the Fleet*
6. *The Purple Rose of Cairo*		**f.**	*Camille* (1937)
7. *L.A. Confidential*		**g.**	*The Philadelphia Story*
8. *Hannah and Her Sisters*		**h.**	*Gold Diggers of 1933*
9. *Twelve Monkeys*		**i.**	*Now, Voyager*
10. *Pennies from Heaven*		**j.**	*Touch of Evil*

200. Match the film about movie people on the left to the fictional film on the right that is part of its story (some of these made-up films are glimpsed and some are just referred to). The clues under the actual films should help a little.

1. *A Star Is Born* (1937)
   Vicki Lester's Oscar-
   winning performance.

   a. *The Longest Night*

2. *A Star Is Born* (1954)
   Vicki Lester's Oscar-
   winning performance.

   b. *The Doom of the Cat Men*

3. *The Bad and the
   "Beautiful*
   One of Jonathan
   Shields's early films.

   c. *Hearts and Pearls*

4. *Singin' in the Rain*
   The film that premieres
   in the first scene.

   d. *A World for Two*

5. *Sullivan's Travels*
   The director's dream
   project.

   e. *The Fatal Winter*

6. *Silk Stockings*
   One of Peggy Dayton's
   swimming pictures.

   f. *O Brother, Where Art Thou?*

7. *What Ever Happened
   to Baby Jane?*
   One of Jane's flops.

   g. *Swinging Down to Panama*

8. *The Band Wagon*
   One of Tony Hunter's
   old musicals.

   h. *Dream Without End*

9. *The Star*
   Margaret Elliot tests
   for this film.

   i. *Neptune's Mother*

10. *Sherlock Jr.*
    The film the projectionist
    enters into.

    j. *The Royal Rascal*

THE ANSWERS

1.

1. c
2. j
3. h
4. a
5. e

6. g
7. i
8. d
9. f
10. b

2.

1. h
2. b
3. i
4. g
5. a

6. j
7. c
8. e
9. d
10. f

3.

1. c (Gene Tierney)
2. h (Audrey Hepburn)
3. e (no one)
4. a (Rita Hayworth)
5. j (Tippi Hedren)

6. d (Jeanne Crain)
7. i (Leslie Caron)
8. b (Jean Simmons)
9. g (Sue Lyon)
10. f (Jeanne Crain)

4.

1. b (Gary Cooper)
2. h (James Stewart)
3. e (Joel McCrea)
4. j (Henry Fonda)
5. c (Roland Young)

6. i (James Stewart)
7. f (Walter Huston)
8. d (Colin Clive)
9. g (Gary Cooper)
10. a (Errol Flynn)

5.

1. e	6. j
2. a	7. d
3. g	8. h
4. f	9. c
5. b	10. i

6.

1. h	6. e
2. d	7. i
3. f	8. c
4. j	9. a
5. b	10. g

7.

1. g	6. f
2. e	7. j
3. i	8. d
4. b	9. h
5. c	10. a

8.

1. h	6. b
2. c	7. i
3. e	8. d
4. a	9. j
5. g	10. f

9.

1. i	6. j
2. d	7. b
3. a	8. g
4. f	9. e
5. c	10. h

10.

1. f	6. i
2. a	7. b
3. h	8. g
4. j	9. e
5. d	10. c

11.

1. c	6. i
2. h	7. j
3. d	8. b
4. a	9. g
5. f	10. e

12.

1. d (*The Glass Menagerie*)
2. h (*Suddenly, Last Summer*)
3. f (*The Fugitive Kind*)
4. a (*The Roman Spring of Mrs. Stone*)
5. c (*The Fugitive Kind*)
6. j (*The Night of the Iguana*)
7. b (*The Night of the Iguana*)
8. i (*Sweet Bird of Youth*)
9. e (*Sweet Bird of Youth*)
10. g (*Boom!*)

13.

1. e	6. a
2. h	7. d
3. b	8. i
4. j	9. c
5. g	10. f

14.

1. e (*Devotion*)
2. i (*Magnificent Doll*)
3. b (*Beloved Infidel*)
4. a (*I Want to Live!*)
5. g (*Young Bess*)
6. j (*Sister Kenny*)
7. h (*The Barretts of Wimpole Street*—1957)
8. f (*The Great Ziegfeld*)
9. c (*The Plainsman*)
10. d (*Sunrise at Campobello*)

15.

    1. g *(The Gorgeous Hussy)*
    2. d *(Rembrandt)*
    3. j *(Edison, the Man)*
    4. e *(Dr. Ehrlich's Magic Bullet)*
    5. a *(Juarez)*
    6. c *(Viva Villa!)*
    7. h *(The Spirit of St. Louis)*
    8. b *(The Adventures of Mark Twain)*
    9. i *(The Story of G.I. Joe)*
  10. f *(Magnificent Doll)*

16.

    1. h (the murdered little boy)
    2. d (the father's mistress)
    3. g (Mary's cheating husband)
    4. b (the letter writer)
    5. j (the family patriarch)
    6. a (the murdered model)
    7. e (the beau Blanche is expecting)
    8. c (Mrs. Anna's dead husband)
    9. f (Brigid's partner-in-crime)
  10. i (father of the sextuplets)

17.

    1. h   6. i
    2. e   7. a
    3. b   8. f
    4. j   9. d
    5. c   10. g

18.

    1. e (Gregory Peck)
    2. d (Joan Crawford)
    3. i (Robert Montgomery)
    4. b (Carole Lombard)
    5. h (Rock Hudson)
    6. c (Claudette Colbert)
    7. a (May Robson)
    8. g (Joel McCrea)
    9. f (Jean Arthur)
  10. j (Joel McCrea)

19.

1. g	6. j
2. c	7. e
3. h	8. a
4. f	9. b
5. d	10. i

Note: Gig Young took his character's name as his professional name. He had been known as Byron Barr.

20.

1. a	6. a
2. c	7. d
3. d	8. d
4. b	9. b
5. b	10. c

21.

1. c	6. d
2. h	7. b
3. f	8. e
4. a	9. g
5. j	10. i

22.

1. e	6. b
2. c	7. i
3. h	8. f
4. a	9. g
5. j	10. d

23.

1. h	6. b
2. c	7. d
3. j	8. i
4. a	9. g
5. e	10. f

24.

1. e	6. d
2. h	7. i
3. b	8. f
4. j	9. c
5. a	10. g

25.

1. d *(The Magnificent Ambersons)*
2. g *(Jezebel)*
3. j *(The Wizard of Oz)*
4. a *(Arsenic and Old Lace)*
5. h *(A Tree Grows in Brooklyn)*
6. c *(The Heiress)*
7. e *(The Little Foxes)*
8. b *(Little Women)*
9. f *(Gone With the Wind)*
10. i *(Oklahoma!)*

26.

1. e	6. c
2. g	7. i
3. a	8. d
4. f	9. h
5. j	10. b

27.

1. i (Douglas)
2. d (Stewart)
3. f (Cagney, brother/sister)
4. e (Mills, daughter/father)
5. a (Kerr)
6. b (Barrymore, brothers)
7. h (Taylor)
8. c (Taylor)
9. g (Ladd, father/son)
10. j (Davis)

28.

1. c	6. f
2. i	7. h
3. d	8. e
4. g	9. a
5. j	10. b

29.

1. f	6. b
2. i	7. j
3. a	8. e
4. d	9. h
5. g	10. c

30.

1. f	6. d
2. i	7. j
3. b	8. c
4. a	9. e
5. h	10. g

31.

1. e	6. j
2. a	7. h
3. d	8. i
4. c	9. f
5. b	10. g

32.

1. g	6. j
2. f	7. b
3. a	8. d
4. h	9. i
5. c	10. e

33.

    1. i (*The Adventures of Robin Hood*)
    2. e (*Anna and the King of Siam*)
    3. b (*Robin Hood*)
    4. a (*Forever Amber* and *The King's Thief*)
    5. g (*The Three Musketeers*)
    6. d (*Tower of London*)
    7. j (*Knights of the Round Table*)
    8. c (*Marie Antoinette*)
    9. f (*Becket* and *The Lion in Winter*)
    10. h (*Henry V*)

34.

    1. d (*Young Bess*)
    2. g (*Adventures of Don Juan*)
    3. i (*The Lion in Winter*)
    4. a (*Salome*)
    5. e (*Rasputin and the Empress*)
    6. b (*Fire Over England* and *The Sea Hawk*)
    7. j (*Knights of the Round Table*)
    8. f (*The Private Life of Henry VIII*)
    9. h (*The Mudlark*)
    10. c (*The Three Musketeers*)

35.

    1. b (ranch)
    2. a (plantation)
    3. g (ranch)
    4. j (plantation)
    5. d (house)
    6. c (estate)
    7. i (psychiatric institution)
    8. e (psychiatric institution)
    9. f (fishing lodge)
    10. h (estate)

36.

1. f	6. i
2. j	7. e
3. a	8. d
4. h	9. g
5. c	10. b

37.

1. c	6. d
2. e	7. j
3. i	8. h
4. f	9. g
5. a	10. b

38.

1. j	6. i
2. a	7. f
3. e	8. b
4. h	9. g
5. c	10. d

39.

1. f	6. d
2. i	7. j
3. b	8. h
4. g	9. e
5. a	10. c

40.

1. i	6. a
2. d	7. e
3. b	8. j
4. f	9. g
5. h	10. c

Note: Lew Ayres was a conscientious objector who served with the Army Medical Corps and also as an assistant chaplain.

41.

1. e	6. a
2. h	7. c
3. b	8. i
4. j	9. f
5. d	10. g

42.

1. f	6. j
2. d	7. c
3. i	8. e
4. a	9. g
5. h	10. b

43.

1. g	6. i
2. e	7. j
3. a	8. b
4. d	9. c
5. h	10. f

44.

1. e	6. b
2. h	7. c
3. a	8. i
4. d	9. f
5. j	10. g

45.

1. j	6. a
2. g	7. c
3. b	8. i
4. f	9. d
5. e	10. h

46.

1. f (Anne Welles)
2. i (title role)
3. e (Susan Alexander)
4. c (Aron Trask)
5. j (title role)
6. h (blind girl)
7. a (Joey Drayton)
8. g (Eddie Kerns)
9. d (Carl Denham)
10. b (Michael Rossi)

47.

1. d
2. i
3. g
4. e
5. a
6. h
7. b
8. j
9. f
10. c

48.

1. e
2. d
3. a
4. i
5. g
6. c
7. j
8. h
9. b
10. f

49.

1. h *(The Public Enemy)*
2. j *(Champion)*
3. d *(Four Daughters)*
4. i *(This Gun for Hire)*
5. b *(Golden Boy)*
6. g *(The Killers)*
7. e *(High Sierra)*
8. a *(Kiss of Death)*
9. c *(East of Eden)*
10. f *(Splendor in the Grass)*

50.

1. a *(To Have and Have Not)*
2. j *(The Outlaw)*
3. h *(Picnic)*
4. c *(The Killers)*
5. f *(Goodbye, Mr. Chips)*
6. i *(Blood and Sand)*
7. b *(The Jungle Princess)*
8. e *(Intermezzo)*
9. d *(She Done Him Wrong)*
10. g *(Niagara)*

51.

1. c
2. f
3. d
4. i
5. b
6. a
7. h
8. e
9. j
10. g

52.

1. i
2. e
3. h
4. a
5. c
6. d
7. j
8. f
9. b
10. g

53.

1. d
2. g
3. b
4. i
5. a
6. c
7. j
8. f
9. e
10. h

54.

1. GG (*Anna Karenina*—1935)
2. LG
3. LG
4. LG (*The Night of the Hunter*—1955)
5. GG
6. LG
7. GG
8. GG (*Anna Christie*—1930)
9. GG
10. LG

55.

1. NS (*The Barretts of Wimpole Street*—1934)
2. GG (*Pride and Prejudice*—1940)
3. NS
4. NS (*Romeo and Juliet*—1936)
5. GG (*Julius Caesar*—1953)
6. GG (*The Miniver Story*—1950, the sequel to *Mrs. Miniver*—1942)
7. NS
8. GG (*Blossoms in the Dust*—1941; *Mrs. Miniver*—1942; *Madame Curie*—1943; *Mrs. Parkington*—1944; *The Valley of Decision*—1945)
9. NS
10. GG

56.

1. JC
2. BD (*Of Human Bondage*)
3. JC (*Daisy Kenyon*—1947)
4. BD (*June Bride*)
5. BD
6. JC (*Mildred Pierce*)
7. JC
8. BD
9. BD
10. JC (*Susan and God*)

57.

    1. JA
    2. CL
    3. CL
    4. JA
    5. CL *(Mr. and Mrs. Smith)*
    6. JA *(The Whole Town's Talking)*
    7. CL
    8. CL
    9. JA
  10. JA

58.

    1. IL
    2. BS
    3. BS
    4. IL
    5. BS
    6. BS
    7. IL
    8. BS *(Night Nurse*—1931; *To Please a Lady*—1950)
    9. IL
  10. IL

59.

    1. JM (same title—1941)
    2. JM
    3. AF
    4. JM *(I Married an Angel)*
    5. JM *(Bitter Sweet)*
    6. AF *(In Old Chicago*—1937)
    7. AF
    8. AF
    9. JM
  10. AF

60.

1. JF
2. OD
3. OD (*My Cousin Rachel*)
4. OD
5. OD (*A Midsummer Night's Dream*—1935)
6. JF
7. OD
8. JF
9. JF (*A Damsel in Distress*—1937)
10. JF (*The Emperor Waltz*—1948, Crosby; *Serenade*—1956, Lanza)

61.

1. JW
2. JW (*Stage Fright*)
3. LY (*The Stranger*)
4. LY
5. LY
6. JW
7. LY
8. JW
9. LY (*Four Men and a Prayer*—1938; *Three Blind Mice*—1938; *Eternally Yours*—1939; *The Perfect Marriage*—1946; *The Bishop's Wife*—1947)
10. JW (*The Lost Weekend*—1945)

62.

1. LT (*Honky Tonk*—1941; *Somewhere I'll Find You*—1942; *Homecoming*—1948; *Betrayed*—1954)
2. AG (*The Barefoot Contessa*)
3. LT (*The Bad and the Beautiful*)
4. LT (*The Rains of Ranchipur*)
5. LT (*Weekend at the Waldorf*—1945)
6. AG
7. AG (*Mogambo*—1953)
8. LT
9. AG
10. AG (*One Touch of Venus*—1948)

63.

1. AH (*Roman Holiday*—1953)
2. AH (*The Nun's Story*—1959)
3. AH (*My Fair Lady*—1964, a remake of *Pygmalion*—1938)
4. GK (*Mogambo*—1953, a remake of *Red Dust*)
5. AH (*Love in the Afternoon*—1957)
6. GK
7. GK ("True Love" from *High Society*)
8. GK (*Mogambo*—1953)
9. AH (*Roman Holiday*—1953; *The Children's Hour*—1961; *How to Steal a Million*—1966)
10. GK (*The Swan*)

64.

1. f	6. g
2. c	7. j
3. a	8. b
4. i	9. h
5. d	10. e

65.

1. d	6. c
2. f	7. e
3. h	8. b
4. a	9. j
5. i	10. g

66.

1. c	6. i
2. h	7. e
3. f	8. j
4. b	9. g
5. a	10. d

67.

1. j	6. h
2. e	7. f
3. a	8. b
4. i	9. c
5. g	10. d

68.

1. j	6. c
2. h	7. d
3. g	8. b
4. f	9. e
5. i	10. a

69.

1. f	6. e
2. a	7. b
3. h	8. d
4. c	9. i
5. j	10. g

70.

1. f	6. g
2. b	7. j
3. i	8. d
4. c	9. h
5. a	10. e

71.

1. h	6. a
2. e	7. f
3. d	8. b
4. g	9. c
5. j	10. i

72.

1. d	6. c
2. a	7. j
3. i	8. e
4. f	9. b
5. h	10. g

73.

1. e	6. d
2. h	7. i
3. c	8. f
4. j	9. b
5. a	10. g

74.

1. a	6. e
2. h	7. j
3. d	8. f
4. i	9. g
5. c	10. b

75.

1. i	6. j
2. f	7. c
3. h	8. a
4. b	9. e
5. g	10. d

76.

1. b	6. c
2. e	7. j
3. g	8. d
4. a	9. h
5. i	10. f

77.

1. c	6. j
2. e	7. i
3. d	8. f
4. g	9. a
5. h	10. b

78.

1. g	6. d
2. c	7. h
3. e	8. b
4. a	9. j
5. i	10. f

79.

1. g
2. i
3. d
4. b
5. h

6. j
7. e
8. a
9. f
10. c

Note: *That Night in Rio* and *On the Riviera* are both remakes of the 1935 *Folies Bergère* starring Maurice Chevalier.

80.

1. e
2. h
3. a
4. c
5. g

6. b
7. j
8. d
9. f
10. i

81.

1. c
2. g
3. i
4. a
5. j

6. d
7. f
8. e
9. b
10. h

82.

1. g
2. c
3. d
4. i
5. f

6. e
7. a
8. b
9. j
10. h

83.

1. c
2. d
3. j
4. a
5. g

6. i
7. f
8. h
9. b
10. e

84.

1. h
2. e
3. c
4. g
5. i

6. a
7. f
8. j
9. d
10. b

85.

1. b (*Bachelor Mother; Magnificent Doll; Oh, Men! Oh, Women!*)
2. i (*Phffft; Bell, Book and Candle; The Notorious Landlady*)
3. e (*Wings in the Dark; The Bachelor and the Bobby-Soxer; Mr. Blandings Builds His Dream House*)
4. g (*Of Human Bondage; The Petrified Forest; It's Love I'm After*)
5. d (*Gaslight; Arch of Triumph; A Matter of Time*)
6. c (*The Stratton Story; The Glenn Miller Story; Strategic Air Command*)
7. a (*East Side, West Side; Pandora and the Flying Dutchman; Mayerling*)
8. h (*Crash Dive; The Razor's Edge; The Luck of the Irish*)
9. j (*Jamaica Inn; The Hunchback of Notre Dame; This Land Is Mine*)
10. f (*Angel Face; She Couldn't Say No; The Grass Is Greener*)

86.

    1. c *(Pillow Talk; Lover Come Back; Send Me No Flowers)*

    2. i *(Woman of the Year; Keeper of the Flame; Without Love; The Sea of Grass; State of the Union; Adam's Rib; Pat and Mike; Desk Set; Guess Who's Coming to Dinner)*

    3. f *(Arabian Nights; White Savage; Ali Baba and the Forty Thieves; Cobra Woman; Gypsy Wildcat; Sudan)*

    4. a *(To Catch a Thief)*

    5. h *(Dance, Fools, Dance; Laughing Sinners; Possessed; Dancing Lady; Chained; Forsaking All Others; Love on the Run; Strange Cargo)*

    6. d *(Next Time We Love; The Shopworn Angel; The Shop Around the Corner; The Mortal Storm)*

    7. g *(The Gilded Lily; The Bride Comes Home; Maid of Salem; No Time for Love; Practically Yours; The Egg and I; Family Honeymoon)*

    8. b *(The Apartment; Irma La Douce)*

    9. e *(Ladies in Love; Love Is News; Café Metropole; Second Honeymoon; Suez)*

  10. j *(Flying Down to Rio; The Gay Divorcée; Roberta; Top Hat; Follow the Fleet; Swing Time; Shall We Dance; Carefree; The Story of Vernon and Irene Castle; The Barkleys of Broadway)*

87.

1. a	6. i
2. j	7. b
3. h	8. d
4. f	9. g
5. c	10. e

88.

1. c	6. b
2. a	7. c
3. b	8. d
4. c	9. a
5. a	10. d

Note: Gene Kelly played D'Artagnan in *The Three Musketeers.*

89.

1. g	6. j
2. d	7. i
3. e	8. f
4. a	9. b
5. c	10. h

90.

1. g (Irving Berlin)
2. c (Richard Rodgers and Lorenz Hart)
3. h (Jerome Kern and Ira Gershwin)
4. a (Burton Lane and Ralph Freed)
5. j (Cole Porter)
6. b (Irving Berlin)
7. i (George and Ira Gershwin)
8. e (George and Ira Gershwin)
9. d (Harry Warren and Al Dubin)
10. f (Harry Warren and Al Dubin)

91.

1. a (Harry Warren and Mack Gordon)
2. f (Con Conrad and Herb Magidson)
3. i (Ray Evans and Jay Livingston)
4. g (Ray Evans and Jay Livingston)
5. b (Jerome Kern and Oscar Hammerstein)
6. j (Ralph Rainger and Leo Robin)
7. e (Jerome Kern and Dorothy Fields)
8. d (James Van Heusen and Johnny Burke)
9. c (James Van Heusen and Sammy Cahn)
10. h (Hoagy Carmichael and Johnny Mercer)

92.

1. d	6. b
2. f	7. e
3. h	8. c
4. a	9. g
5. j	10. i

93.

1. c	6. f
2. g	7. b
3. a	8. d
4. e	9. j
5. h	10. i

94.

1. d	6. b
2. g	7. e
3. a	8. f
4. i	9. h
5. c	10. j

95.

1. h	6. e
2. f	7. a
3. j	8. g
4. b	9. i
5. d	10. c

96.

1. b	6. d
2. e	7. j
3. i	8. c
4. a	9. h
5. g	10. f

97.

1. c	6. a
2. e	7. d
3. i	8. g
4. h	9. f
5. j	10. b

98.

1. c	6. d
2. f	7. e
3. i	8. g
4. a	9. j
5. h	10. b

99.

1. e
2. a
3. h
4. c
5. f

6. i
7. b
8. d
9. g
10. j

100.

1. d
2. g
3. i
4. e
5. j

6. c
7. b
8. a
9. f
10. h

101.

1. g
2. c
3. i
4. e
5. d

6. h
7. a
8. j
9. b
10. f

102.

1. e
2. f
3. b
4. d
5. j

6. c
7. i
8. a
9. g
10. h

103.

1. b
2. i
3. g
4. c
5. h

6. a
7. e
8. j
9. f
10. d

104.

1. d
2. e
3. g
4. i
5. c

6. h
7. j
8. f
9. b
10. a

105.

1. h	6. d
2. e	7. j
3. b	8. c
4. a	9. g
5. i	10. f

106.

1. e	6. a
2. c	7. d
3. i	8. j
4. h	9. b
5. f	10. g

107.

1. d	6. f
2. g	7. i
3. a	8. e
4. j	9. b
5. c	10. h

108.

1. h (Herman J. Mankiewicz and Orson Welles)
2. e
3. a (Luise Rainer)
4. j
5. c (Spencer Tracy)
6. d (John Ford)
7. i (Leo McCarey)
8. g
9. f
10. b (Frank Capra)

109.

1. b	6. a
2. c	7. d
3. b	8. d
4. c	9. b
5. a	10. a

110.

1. d (1958)
2. d (1964)
3. c (1952)
4. a (1939)
5. b (1943)

6. d (1956)
7. a (1948)
8. b (1945)
9. c (1954)
10. a (1968)

111.

1. d (1952)
2. a (1942)
3. b (1942)
4. c (1951)
5. b (1946)

6. a (1954)
7. c (1941)
8. d (1945)
9. c (1948)
10. a (1944)

112.

1. b (1957)
2. a (1953)
3. a (1945)
4. d (1956)
5. c (1936)

6. a (1958)
7. b (1943)
8. c (1945)
9. c (1941)
10. d (1947)

Note: Mitchum and Perkins were nominated in the
supporting category.

113.

1. i (*The Towering Inferno*)
2. j (*Victor/Victoria*)
3. e (*Giant*)
4. b (*Abe Lincoln in Illinois*)
5. a (*The Awful Truth*)
6. d (*Broken Arrow*)
7. c (*A Song to Remember*)
8. h (*Ryan's Daughter*)
9. f (*Sons and Lovers*)
10. g (*The Sand Pebbles*)

Mills was the only winner.

114.

   1. h (*Summer Wishes, Winter Dreams*)
   2. g (*Days of Wine and Roses*)
   3. d (*Duel in the Sun*)
   4. e (*The Blue Veil*)
   5. i (*A Passage to India*)
   6. b (*The Dark Angel*)
   7. j (*The Whales of August*)
   8. c (*Our Town*)
   9. a (*Morocco*)
10. f (*Baby Doll*)
Ashcroft was the only winner.

115.

   1. d (1942)
   2. i (1936)
   3. b (1930–31)
   4. h (1932–33)
   5. j (1950)
   6. g (1967)
   7. a (1944)
   8. e (1943)
   9. c (1954)
10. f (1934)

Lukas was the only winner.

116.

   1. c (*Gaslight*—1944)
   2. g (*The Miracle Worker*—1962)
   3. j (*The Country Girl*—1954)
   4. e (*Guess Who's Coming to Dinner*—1967)
   5. b (*Come Back, Little Sheba*—1952)
   6. i (*On the Waterfront*—1954)
   7. a (*Butterfield 8*—1960)
   8. d (*It Happened One Night*—1934)
   9. f (*The Heiress*—1949)
10. h (*Written on the Wind*—1956)
Note: Malone and Saint won in the supporting category.

117.

   1. j (1941)
   2. d (1966)
   3. f (1959)
   4. e (1955)
   5. c (1963)
   6. a (1945)
   7. b (1950)
   8. i (1948)
   9. h (1929–30)
10. g (1949)

118.

1. h (1948)
2. a (1957)
3. f (1950)
4. c (1927–28)
5. i (1940)
6. e (1932–33)
7. b (1935)
8. j (1947)
9. d (1945)
10. g (1929–30)

119.

1. e (*Suspicion*—1941)
2. c (*Kentucky*—1938)
3. h (*Goodbye, Mr. Chips*—1969; Robert Donat won in 1939)
4. f (*Sabrina*)
5. a (1941 nomination for *Hold Back the Dawn,* but lost to Joan Fontaine in *Suspicion*)
6. g (*Abe Lincoln in Illinois*—1940; Daniel Massey was nominated for his Noël Coward in *Star!*—1968)
7. i (*Champion*—1949; *Bright Victory*—1951; *Trial*—1955; *Peyton Place*—1957; all directed by Mark Robson)
8. d (*The Happy Ending*—1969; directed by Richard Brooks)
9. j (Henry VIII in *Anne of the Thousand Days*—1969; Laughton won for *The Private Life of Henry VIII*—1932–33)
10. b (*Summertime*—1955)

120.

1. d (*Lovely to Look At*)
2. e (*An Affair to Remember*)
3. j (*Always*)
4. a (*Let's Do It Again*)
5. c (*Move Over, Darling*)
6. h (same title)
7. i (same title)
8. g (*Interlude*)
9. f (same title)
10. b (same title)

121.

1. c
2. f
3. i
4. a
5. e

6. j
7. d
8. b
9. h
10. g

122.

1. g
2. h
3. i
4. a
5. e

6. c
7. j
8. b
9. d
10. f

123.

1. i (*Two Girls on Broadway*)
2. f (same title)
3. d (*Congo Maisie*)
4. e (*Easy to Wed*)
5. j (same title)
6. g (*Satan Met a Lady*)
7. b (same title)
8. a (*Castle on the Hudson*)
9. h (same title)
10. c (*A Place in the Sun*)

124.

1. d (*The Barretts of Wimpole Street*)
2. a (*A Star Is Born*)
3. h (*Pygmalion/My Fair Lady*)
4. b (*Goodbye, Mr. Chips*)
5. g (*The Philadelphia Story/High Society*)
6. c (*Ninotchka/Silk Stockings*)
7. e (*Red Dust/Mogambo*)
8. f (*Mutiny on the Bounty*)
9. i (*The Shop Around the Corner/In the Good Old Summertime*)
10. j (*The Champ*)

125.

    1. e (*Walk, Don't Run*)
    2. h (*The Life and Times of Judge Roy Bean*)
    3. a (same title)
    4. c (Cisco Kid series)
    5. j (*High Society*)
    6. g (*The Mudlark*)
    7. d (*The Girl Who Had Everything*)
    8. f (*A Man for All Seasons*)
    9. b (*You Can't Run Away from It*)
    10. i (same title)

126.

1. b		6. i
2. e		7. a
3. j		8. d
4. g		9. f
5. c		10. h

127.

    1. f (*Summer Holiday*)
    2. c (*A Song Is Born*)
    3. i (*You Can't Run Away from It*)
    4. a (*Bundle of Joy*)
    5. j (*The Girl Most Likely*)
    6. d (*Masquerade in Mexico*)
    7. g (*Three for the Show*)
    8. e (*I'll Be Yours*)
    9. b (*About Face*)
    10. h (*The Chocolate Soldier*)
Note: MGM replaced the *Arms and the Man* plot with *The Guardsman*'s plot when they made *The Chocolate Soldier* into a film.

128.

1. f		6. j
2. h		7. e
3. b		8. d
4. a		9. i
5. c		10. g

129.

1. d	6. h
2. f	7. j
3. b	8. e
4. i	9. g
5. a	10. c

130.

1. f *(Mrs. Miniver/The Miniver Story)*
2. d *(Father of the Bride/Father's Little Dividend)*
3. j (Dr. Kildare series)
4. a (Andy Hardy series)
5. h *(Boys Town/Men of Boys Town)*
6. g *(Jesse James/The Return of Frank James)*
7. b *(Dear Ruth/Dear Wife)*
8. c *(The Thin Man* series)
9. e *(See Here, Private Hargrove/What Next, Corporal Hargrove?)*
10. i *(On Moonlight Bay/By the Light of the Silvery Moon)*

131.

1. a	6. d
2. g	7. h
3. e	8. f
4. j	9. c
5. b	10. i

132.

1. i	6. c
2. e	7. j
3. b	8. f
4. g	9. d
5. a	10. h

133.

1. e (team)
2. c (LeRoy replaced Ford)
3. i (team)
4. a (team)
5. h (team)
6. j (team)
7. b (Wyler replaced Hawks)
8. d (team)
9. g (team)
10. f (Curtiz replaced Keighley)

134.

1. e	6. a
2. j	7. f
3. g	8. d
4. b	9. h
5. i	10. c

135.

1. i	6. c
2. f	7. h
3. e	8. j
4. g	9. d
5. a	10. b

136.

1. d (*Sunset Boulevard; Stalag 17; Sabrina; Fedora*)
2. g (*Romance on the High Seas; My Dream Is Yours; Young Man With a Horn; I'll See You in My Dreams*)
3. j (*The Plainsman; North West Mounted Police; The Story of Dr. Wassell; Unconquered*)
4. f (*Babes in Arms; Strike Up the Band; Babes on Broadway; For Me and My Gal*)
5. h (*The Ghost and Mrs. Muir; Escape; Cleopatra; The Honey Pot*)
6. i (*Man Hunt; The Woman in the Window; Scarlet Street; Secret Beyond the Door*)
7. c (*Rope; Rear Window; The Man Who Knew Too Much; Vertigo*)
8. a (*Ladies of Leisure; The Miracle Woman; Forbidden; The Bitter Tea of General Yen; Meet John Doe*)
9. b (*These Three; The Heiress; Carrie; The Children's Hour*)
10. e (*The Love Parade; Monte Carlo; One Hour With You; The Merry Widow*)

Note: James Stewart and Frank Capra made only 3 films together.

137.

1. d	6. a
2. j	7. i
3. h	8. g
4. b	9. c
5. e	10. f

138.

1. d	6. c
2. j	7. a
3. b	8. f
4. g	9. h
5. i	10. e

139.

1. g	6. b
2. e	7. a
3. h	8. d
4. i	9. c
5. f	10. j

140.

1. j	6. a
2. e	7. i
3. h	8. c
4. b	9. f
5. d	10. g

141.

1. f	6. b
2. g	7. d
3. i	8. j
4. a	9. c
5. h	10. e

142.

1. c	6. g
2. e	7. j
3. i	8. f
4. a	9. d
5. b	10. h

143.

1. c	6. h
2. f	7. b
3. i	8. j
4. a	9. e
5. d	10. g

144.

1. a	6. j
2. e	7. f
3. h	8. d
4. c	9. g
5. b	10. i

145.

1. e	6. c
2. d	7. j
3. i	8. a
4. b	9. f
5. g	10. h

146.

1. e	6. j
2. d	7. c
3. i	8. f
4. g	9. b
5. a	10. h

147.

1. d	6. e
2. h	7. i
3. f	8. c
4. b	9. g
5. j	10. a

148.

1. c	6. b
2. f	7. i
3. g	8. j
4. a	9. d
5. e	10. h

149.

1. d (Cliff Robertson)
2. f (Gene Tierney)
3. b (Katharine Hepburn—1932; Maureen O'Hara—1940)
4. a (Joan Crawford)
5. h (Gregory Peck)
6. j (Joanne Woodward)
7. e (Olivia de Havilland)
8. g (Katharine Hepburn)
9. c (Claude Rains)
10. i (Anthony Perkins)

150.

1. f (Florence Bates)
2. i (Jessie Royce Landis)
3. e (Elizabeth Taylor)
4. j (Marlene Dietrich)
5. g (Ida Lupino)
6. h (Audrey Hepburn)
7. a (Paul Henreid)
8. c (Susan Hayward)
9. b (Robert Walker)
10. d (William Holden)

151.

1. e (Elizabeth Taylor)
2. g (Tallulah Bankhead)
3. f (Lana Turner)
4. b (Priscilla Lane)
5. i (Ann Dvorak)
6. c (Renee Carson)
7. a (Marlene Dietrich)
8. j (Lana Turner)
9. h (James Mason)
10. d (Angela Scoular)

152.

1. f
2. c
3. a
4. i
5. g
6. e
7. j
8. b
9. h
10. d

153.

1. g
2. i (curtain call)
3. b
4. f
5. a
6. j
7. d
8. h
9. c
10. e

154.

1. f (with Jane Murfin)
2. c (with John Huston)
3. h (with Alan Campbell and Robert Carson)
4. b (with Albert Hackett and Frances Goodrich)
5. j
6. a (with Tennessee Williams)
7. i (with Edward E. Paramore)
8. e (with Jules Furthman)
9. g
10. d (with John Huston)

155.

1. b (Irene Dunne)
2. d (Gene Tierney)
3. g (Auriol Lee)
4. i (Rosalind Russell)
5. a (Charles Boyer)
6. j (Dick Powell)
7. e (Cary Grant)
8. f (the murdered doctor)
9. c (Oscar Homolka)
10. h (Miriam Hopkins)

156.

1. g
2. d
3. i
4. a
5. j
6. e
7. c
8. h
9. b
10. f

157.

1. CC
2. CC (*The Circus*—1927–28)
3. BK
4. BK
5. CC
6. CC (*The Great Dictator*—1940)
7. BK
8. BK
9. CC (*Monsieur Verdoux*)
10. BK

158.

1. HB (*The African Queen*—1951)
2. EGR
3. HB
4. HB (*The Petrified Forest*)
5. EGR (*The Woman in the Window*—1944; *Scarlet Street*—1945)
6. EGR (*The Stranger*—1946)
7. EGR
8. HB
9. EGR
10. HB (*Dead End*—1937; *The Desperate Hours*—1955)

159.

1. ST
2. CG
3. CG (*The Misfits*—1961)
4. CG
5. CG
6. ST
7. ST
8. ST (*The Sea of Grass*—1947)
9. ST
10. CG

160.

1. JS
2. CG (*Once Upon a Honeymoon*—1942; *Monkey Business*—1952)
3. CG
4. JS
5. CG
6. JS (*Rose Marie*—1936)
7. CG (*North by Northwest*—1959)
8. JS
9. JS
10. CG (*The Talk of the Town*)

161.

1. TP	6. TP
2. TP	7. EF
3. EF	8. EF
4. EF	9. EF
5. TP	10. TP

162.

1. JM (*Colorado Territory*—1949)
2. RS (*Roberta*—1935; *Follow the Fleet*—1936)
3. RS
4. JM
5. JM
6. RS (*The Spoilers* and *Pittsburgh*)
7. JM
8. RS
9. JM
10. RS

163.

1. GK
2. GK (*Les Girls*—1957)
3. FA (*Finian's Rainbow*—1968)
4. GK (*The Three Musketeers*)
5. FA (*Yolanda and the Thief*—1945)
6. FA ("The Way You Look Tonight" from *Swing Time*—1936)
7. GK (*For Me and My Gal*—1942)
8. FA (*Royal Wedding*—1951)
9. FA (*Daddy Long Legs*)
10. GK

164.

1. AG	6. LO
2. AG	7. LO
3. LO	8. AG
4. AG	9. LO (*Spartacus*)
5. AG	10. LO

165.

    1. KD (*Ace in the Hole*)
    2. BL (*Trapeze*—1956; *Sweet Smell of Success*—1957)
    3. BL
    4. KD (*The Strange Love of Martha Ivers*—1946)
    5. KD
    6. KD (*The Bad and the Beautiful*—1952; *Lust for Life*—1956; *Two Weeks in Another Town*—1962)
    7. BL (*Elmer Gantry*—1960)
    8. BL (*The Unforgiven*)
    9. BL
    10. KD

166.

    1. MC (*Indiscretion of an American Wife*)
    2. MB (*A Countess from Hong Kong*—1967)
    3. MC (*I Confess*—1953)
    4. MC (*Red River*—1948)
    5. MB (*The Men*—1950)
    6. MB (*Bedtime Story*—1964)
    7. MC (*From Here to Eternity*)
    8. MB (*On the Waterfront*)
    9. MC (*The Misfits*)
    10. MB

167.

1. d	6. b
2. f	7. a
3. i	8. e
4. g	9. j
5. h	10. c

168.

1. c	6. b
2. h	7. i
3. a	8. f
4. g	9. j
5. d	10. e

169.

1. c	6. e
2. a	7. d
3. h	8. i
4. b	9. g
5. j	10. f

170.

1. f (*Dancing Lady*)
2. c (*Broadway Melody of 1940*)
3. b (*Ziegfeld Follies*)
4. j (*Easter Parade*)
5. i (*You Were Never Lovelier*)
6. a (*Swing Time*)
7. d (*Daddy Long Legs*)
8. g (*Royal Wedding*)
9. h (*Silk Stockings*)
10. e (*Funny Face*)

171.

1. a (*Anchors Aweigh*)
2. i (*Brigadoon*)
3. b (*Cover Girl*)
4. e (*Singin' in the Rain*)
5. g (*It's Always Fair Weather*)
6. h (*An American in Paris*)
7. j (*Deep in My Heart*)
8. d (*Ziegfeld Follies*)
9. c (*Anchors Aweigh*)
10. f (*Cover Girl*)

172.

1. f	6. b
2. e	7. d
3. h	8. g
4. j	9. a
5. c	10. i

173.

1. f	6. a
2. h	7. d
3. e	8. c
4. b	9. j
5. i	10. g

174.

1. f	6. g
2. j	7. i
3. e	8. d
4. h	9. b
5. a	10. c

175.

1. g	6. b
2. a	7. e
3. f	8. d
4. i	9. h
5. j	10. c

176.

1. e	6. h
2. d	7. a
3. j	8. b
4. g	9. i
5. c	10. f

177.

1. c	6. e
2. f	7. i
3. g	8. h
4. j	9. a
5. b	10. d

178.

1. i	6. j
2. h	7. g
3. e	8. b
4. c	9. a
5. f	10. d

179.

1. g	6. e
2. d	7. a
3. b	8. f
4. i	9. h
5. c	10. j

180.

1. e	6. a
2. c	7. d
3. i	8. j
4. f	9. g
5. h	10. b

181.

1. g	6. i
2. a	7. b
3. j	8. c
4. f	9. d
5. h	10. e

182.

1. f	6. e
2. i	7. b
3. a	8. j
4. d	9. c
5. g	10. h

183.

1. c	6. e
2. j	7. a
3. f	8. h
4. d	9. g
5. b	10. i

184.

1. c	6. b
2. g	7. a
3. j	8. e
4. i	9. h
5. f	10. d

185.

1. b	6. j
2. d	7. i
3. g	8. h
4. a	9. e
5. c	10. f

186.

1. d	6. c
2. a	7. e
3. i	8. j
4. f	9. b
5. h	10. g

187.

1. i (directed by Luchino Visconti)
2. d (directed by Jean-Luc Godard)
3. h (directed by Luchino Visconti)
4. f (directed by Roberto Rossellini)
5. j (directed by Federico Fellini)
6. b (directed by Michelangelo Antonioni)
7. e (directed by Jean-Luc Godard)
8. c (directed by Jean Renoir)
9. a (directed by Federico Fellini)
10. g (directed by G. W. Pabst)

188.

1. j	6. i
2. g	7. b
3. a	8. c
4. f	9. h
5. d	10. e

189.

1. i (story)
2. f (based on her and Larry Marcus's story)
3. b (based on his original story)
4. a (screenplay)
5. j (screenplay)
6. d (screenplay with Garson Kanin)
7. c (screenplay)
8. g (screenplay with Collier Young)
9. h (his and Gene Kelly's story)
10. e (story idea)

190.

1. c	6. j
2. g	7. b
3. i	8. a
4. d	9. f
5. c	10. h

191.

1. g	6. d
2. c	7. j
3. i	8. b
4. a	9. e
5. h	10. f

Note: Dassin and Leisen also directed. Cole also choreographed.

192.

1. g	6. a
2. d	7. e
3. i	8. j
4. b	9. c
5. h	10. f

193.

1. c	6. i
2. g	7. a
3. h	8. d
4. f	9. e
5. j	10. b

194.

1. f *(W.C. Fields and Me)*
2. c *(Man of a Thousand Faces)*
3. h *(Chaplin)*
4. a *(The Jolson Story/Jolson Sings Again)*
5. g *(Too Much, Too Soon)*
6. d *(The George Raft Story)*
7. j *(The Buster Keaton Story)*
8. b *(The Eddie Cantor Story)*
9. e *(Ed Wood)*
10. i *(Gable and Lombard)*

195.

1. c	6. a
2. b	7. d
3. a	8. b
4. d	9. b
5. c	10. c

196.

1. c	6. c
2. a	7. a
3. d	8. b
4. b	9. d
5. d	10. c

197.

1. b	6. a
2. d	7. c
3. d	8. a
4. a	9. c
5. c	10. b

198.

1. f	6. e
2. d	7. b
3. h	8. c
4. i	9. j
5. a	10. g

199.

1. h	6. a
2. j	7. c
3. i	8. b
4. g	9. d
5. f	10. e

200.

1. h (Janet Gaynor)	6. i (Janis Paige)
2. d (Judy Garland)	7. a (Bette Davis)
3. b (Kirk Douglas)	8. g (Fred Astaire)
4. j	9. e (Bette Davis)
5. f (Joel McCrea)	10. c (Buster Keaton)

SCORE CARD

Points	How Well Did You Do?
0–250	"Sorry, Wrong Number"—It's okay to admit that the only pre-1970 movies you really care about are *The Wizard of Oz* and *It's a Wonderful Life*.
250–500	"To Each His Own"—You probably prefer color to black-and-white, but you do acknowledge that *All About Eve* and *On the Waterfront* are great movies.
500–750	"The Road to Glory"—Nobody has to tell you who Ida Lupino is.
750–1000	"Good News"—You know your stuff, but still can't tell the difference between Arlene Dahl and Rhonda Fleming.
1000–1250	"It's a Gift"—You tend to tape a lot of movies off the TV each week. So many cassettes, so little time.
1250–1500	"Sweet Smell of Success"—Impressive. You certainly mourn the fact that Ann Sheridan didn't get better roles after proving herself in *Kings Row*.
1500–1750	"Magnificent Obsession"—Bravo. You'd rather watch old movies than take a walk in the park on the most beautiful day of the year. You pretend to feel guilty about it.
1750–2000+	"As Good As It Gets"—Move over Gable and Loy, as you are now the new King or Queen of Hollywood. You deserve a star on the Walk of Fame, your footprints in cement, and immediate employment as head of a major studio.